SPARK THE STAGE

Master the Art of Professional Speaking and
Authentic Storytelling to Captivate, Inspire,
and Transform Your Audience

ALEYA HARRIS

Hardcover ISBN: 979-8-9913304-2-8
Paperback ISBN: 979-8-9913304-1-1
Electronic ISBN: 979-8-9913304-0-4
Library of Congress Control: 2024916855

Publishing Consultant: PRESStinely, PRESStinely.com

Portions of this book are works of nonfiction. Certain names and identifying characteristics have been changed.

Printed in the United States of America.

AleyaHarris.com

Disclaimer
Aleya Harris does not claim to cure, prevent, treat or diagnose any medical condition or heal any physical, mental, or emotional ailment. Aleya Harris and her claims have not been evaluated by any government agency or regulatory organization. Should you be concerned about a medical condition, seek advice from a qualified medical professional.

This book is dedicated to my daughter, Ruby Coral.

Thank you for filling my life with joy, mi Colibrí.

Table of Contents

Introduction

In 2019, I began my entrepreneurial journey in an abusive relationship. I was the perfect victim. I was in a job that I hated. I was a sparkly, very cute, pink-lipsticked, round peg in a square hole of blue IBM suits and bald white men. And I couldn't figure my way out. I was lost.

And then I met her. She was running a booth at a convention I attended to sell her services that helped aspiring female entrepreneurs. Her magnetic energy drew people to her booth like the BeyHive to Beyoncé. With each flash of her smile and dramatic gesticulation, she was making bank. I later found out that when she would run booths, she usually walked away with five figures in sales. I saw her and was in awe. She was successful. She was triumphant. She was gorgeous. She was two years into her entrepreneurial journey and had already made over $500,000. She knew what she was doing. So, I asked her for help.

And help I received, but I also reaped the consequences of allowing a narcissistic energy vampire into my life. Every idea she had was better than mine. Every thought and word was better than anything I could ever come up with in my tiny little brain. With each conversation I had with her, I could feel my self-identity and self-respect shrinking. It got to the point where I couldn't send an email or create a presentation without her input and permission.

Together, we built my business.

It was months of constant communication and work until one day, I realized I had a business I didn't know how to run. She had set things up, and she had every step-by-step plan. If there were three steps, she gave me steps one and two, but I had to come back to her for step three. She was more interested in having someone who was an acolyte, not in helping to develop me into a peer or, Lord forbid, someone who could surpass her.

The more time I spent with her, the more I began to see how her initial magnetism was pulling me toward an inner world I didn't want to live in. Every time she spoke, her words dripped with a calculated precision that hinted at an underlying agenda. Her eyes, always scanning the room, seemed to measure the worth of every interaction, calculating how each one could be twisted to her benefit. She had a way of turning compliments into veiled criticisms, making me question my own capabilities. I still remember her saying things like, "That was almost a good idea. Good job! Now here's a better idea…" Of course, after she shared her idea, the conversation would turn back to her. It always did.

Her appearance was polished to perfection—every hair in place, makeup flawlessly applied, and clothes that screamed success. Yet, behind that facade, I could see the subtle signs of her true nature: the tight grip on her phone as she monitored every move of her loved ones, the way her smile never quite reached her eyes, and the dismissive wave of her hand when someone else tried to share their thoughts. She was also a horrible gossip, constantly nitpicking others and tearing them down behind their backs while she complimented them to their faces. She fed off my insecurities and kept me tethered to her control. She had a constant need to overshadow my accomplishments and remind me that without her guidance, I was just another lost soul in the corporate jungle.

I had a business that may have gotten me to that $500,000 mark, but I had no idea what to do with it. And what did that do to me? It made me feel like an impostor. Sometimes, we look around and wonder where our imposter syndrome came from. Mine has a name. At first, I thought it was *her* name, but when I looked into the mirror, I realized it actually was mine.

Like I said, I was playing the perfect victim. I took no accountability for my life. I took no accountability for my situation. I was giving away my agency and looking for someone to save me. I don't know if you've noticed, but there aren't very many knights in shining armor or white horses romping around!

I had to take stock of my situation. I had a business that was supposed to give me all this freedom, and I had none. I had also just gotten laid off. I was lost once again. I had to figure out how to move from the victim place, the place of an impostor, where my voice was not good enough to tell my own story, to where I could step into my power. And I did it in three steps.

The first step was to break up with my mentor. Have you ever broken up with a friend? It just hits different. Just plain rough. I wrote her a letter like I was in the eighth grade. For the record, I did try to talk to her like the mature adult I fancied myself to be. I was a big girl, so I put on my big girl panties and requested a conversation. She said no. If you've ever dealt with a tried and true narcissist, they can't be confronted with any criticism.

Regardless of the awkwardness of the breakup, do you know what I got from that moment? Space. And you know what happens in space? You get to find yourself within that space. I could look at myself and call out the true culprit of the situation. I could see the villain clearly, and she looked like a sparkly, very cute, pink-lipsticked former victim.

There are many victims who did not ask to be victims. But you know who did ask to be a victim? Me. By giving away my agency, by giving away my energetic sovereignty, I put myself in the role of the perfect victim. I had stayed in a victim place with my former business mentor for a long time and I was tired of it. So, I needed to give myself space. And in that space, I started realizing that the only voice equipped to tell my story is my own.

As I moved to the second step of taking responsibility for myself, I realized that I was so far gone that I wasn't even the voice in my own head; she was. I had told mine to take a backseat a long time ago. My next step was to kick her out, to evict her from my head. Then, I had to go and find out who I was, what my true thoughts were, and what I had to say. I had to reconnect with the sound of my inner voice.

It was a profoundly difficult journey. I went to Ayahuasca ceremonies in the Amazon, participated in many seminars, and sat at the feet of a plethora of gurus and coaches. I spent several years trying to do something that should actually be pretty darn easy.

Within all of us, there is a spark, a light. I call it your Radically Authentic Self. It is the undieable part, the part that knows, the part that understands your higher purpose without you having to say anything. It is the part that guides you, the omnipresent part of you made of pure love, pure light. To heal and reach your full potential, all you technically have to do is just uncover that part and connect with it. After that, you'll be fine. Easy peasy, right? Yeah… not so much.

I realized that to uncover my Radically Authentic Self, I didn't have to add anything. I didn't have to get somebody else's voice in my head. I didn't have to read any self-help books (although I did read many). I just needed to unearth the wisdom that I already had. I had to excavate her voice and discard my limiting beliefs and unhelpful programming. Then, I had to replenish myself with uplifting truths.

Once I started to do that, I realized, you know what? I like this Aleya chick. She's pretty dope. What could we create together if I just worked with her? And that was the third and final step on my journey to unearthing and reclaiming myself. I got to creating. Many of the best entrepreneurs already know that they are powerful creators. I was late to the party. I had to take baby steps towards realizing that I had the power within me to create worlds. Once I was able to access that power, I started getting curious. What could I create if it's just little old me?

I created a quarter of a million dollars in six months. I built a business by unearthing that radically authentic part of me, changing the story I told myself, and changing the role I played in that story.

Have you noticed that the hero, the knight, has all the fun in all the classic fairytale stories? He's the one that goes on all the adventures. He slays the dragon, evades the witch, or finds the hidden chalice. He learns about his strengths, his allies, and his potential. He experiences growth. While he is out having the time of his life, the damsel in distress, the victim, is pining away in a tower or just straight-up asleep. It is like her life is on pause until someone can come and save her. I had to get sick and tired of playing the victim role to see any transformation happen and begin my own adventure.

I needed to move from victim to hero. As the radically authentic hero of my story, I get the chance to unearth my power. With that comes the heft of going through crap and making mistakes. But, you know what? I also get to create my happily ever after.

If you've ever felt marginalized, like you couldn't stand in your power, or couldn't tell your own story, I invite you to go on your hero's journey with me in this book. Together, I will help you reacquaint yourself with your inner voice that already knows the way. We will give the eager part of you permission to go on the journey of self-discovery and self-empowerment as you own your story and begin to share it with others so they can also begin their hero's journeys, inspired by how you have navigated yours.

It's time to step out of your comfort zone. That's where the adventure happens. That's where your goals begin to manifest. Yes, you can do this. You can become a professional speaker. We can do this together.

As you step into your power and realize who you are as a powerful creator, I want you to understand that life truly is a fairy tale. It's a fairy tale of your own making. But don't play the damsel in distress. Don't play the one who doesn't step out and use their voice. Play the knight in shining armor. Play the hero role in your own story so that you can guide someone else on theirs. As you step into your power, I invite you today and every day to create your own happily ever after.

After my experience, it became clear to make an impact and reclaim my voice that I had to journey from victim to victor, from silence to speaker. This book is the product of that journey. It's about more than just becoming a professional speaker; it's about transforming your approach to communication and self-perception. Here, you'll discover the practical steps to becoming an engaging speaker and the more profound process of finding and refining your voice.

By embracing the principles of Radically Authentic Strategic Storytelling™, you will learn to convey messages that resonate deeply with others while staying true to yourself. I designed this book to guide you through unearthing your voice, one that's been perhaps silenced or overshadowed by others' expectations or past experiences, much like mine was. Together, we will explore how to articulate your unique stories and insights in a way that captures attention and inspires and mobilizes your audience.

This book equips you with the tools to change how you speak and how you think about yourself and your message. You'll learn to stand confidently in your truth, harness your personal power, and deliver speeches that don't just communicate ideas—they spark change. This is your invitation to step out of the shadows and into the spotlight—not as the person you've been told to be but as the person you are meant to be. Right here is where your speaking journey begins. You'll discover that your voice, once fully unleashed, has the power to reshape your world.

Why Reading This Book Will Transform Your Speaking Journey

If you've ever dreamed of captivating an audience with confidence and ease, understanding that every word you speak has the power to inspire and transform, then you're in the right place. This book is your mentor on the journey toward becoming a profoundly compelling speaker. Through the pages of this book, you'll embark on a transformational path—from feeling uncertain and anxious about public speaking to standing confidently on any stage, empowered by your own voice and story.

Many aspiring speakers grapple with doubts about their ability to engage and influence an audience. These doubts are often compounded by fears of judgment and a lack of confidence, which can keep you from sharing your unique insights and gifts with the world. The challenge of not knowing where to begin or how to structure a compelling speech can make the journey seem daunting. However, I believe every person has a story that deserves to be heard, and it is a profound disservice to yourself and your potential audience to let these fears silence you.

In this book, you'll find practical advice and strategies to overcome these hurdles. You'll learn the foundational principles of Radically Authentic Strategic Storytelling™ and how to connect deeply with your audience. Through detailed exercises, real-world examples, and step-by-step guidance, you'll develop the skills to explore your voice, structure your speeches, and harness your authentic self to engage with others powerfully.

Most importantly, you'll be encouraged to put these skills into practice and craft your own Radical Spark Signature Talk™. Whether you're aiming to inspire a small community group or a large corporate audience, the tools you'll gain from this book will prepare you to confidently step into the spotlight.

A Radical Spark Signature Talk™ is a transformative speaking format designed to unleash the genuine and profound impact of every speaker's personal story and insights. Unlike traditional keynotes or speaking structures that often rely on generic templates and surface-level engagement, the Radical Spark Signature Talk™ delves deep into the essence of Radically Authentic Strategic Storytelling™. This approach encourages speakers to connect with their core truths and express them in a manner that resonates deeply with their audience, making every presentation not just heard but felt.

The critical difference lies in its foundational focus on authenticity and transformation. While conventional speeches might aim to inform or entertain, a Radical Spark Signature Talk™ aims to ignite change—both in the speaker and the audience. It guides speakers through a structured yet flexible process that encourages them to explore and articulate their unique perspectives and experiences. This method fosters a powerful emotional connection with the audience, compelling them to engage more deeply and reflect on their own journeys. By focusing on radical authenticity, this speaking structure ensures that each talk is memorable and a catalyst for personal and collective growth, setting it apart as a beacon of inspiration and actionable insight in the world of professional speaking.

This book also serves as a mirror reflecting your potential and a window offering a view into the techniques that can elevate your speaking. By the end of your journey through these pages, you'll have a toolkit of practical skills and a transformed perspective on what it means to be a speaker. You'll no longer see speaking as just delivering a presentation but as a chance to enact real change—to motivate, uplift, and transform your audience.

By choosing to read this book, you're not just learning how to speak—you're learning how to resonate, influence, and lead. Don't miss the opportunity to turn your speaking ambitions into reality and move from dreaming about giving impactful speeches to actually doing it. Join countless others who have found their voice and their confidence on these pages. Embrace the journey of becoming a speaker, a beacon of inspiration, and a catalyst for change.

Why Being a Professional Speaker Is a Smart Move

Stepping onto the stage as a professional speaker can be thrilling. It's more than just sharing knowledge; it's about delivering performances that captivate and engage your audience, making each experience memorable and impactful. Becoming a professional speaker lets you profoundly impact others. It's not just about being in the spotlight; it's about using that platform to deliver value and share insights and stories that can significantly alter someone's perspective or life. Every time you speak, you have the opportunity to inspire change and contribute positively to others, which can be immensely satisfying.

Speaking professionally also lets you establish yourself as a thought leader. It's not just what you know; it's how you share it and connect with your audience. Each engagement helps to build your brand, showcasing your expertise and solidifying your reputation as the go-to authority on your topics. This recognition can open doors to new collaborations and expand your professional network.

On the financial side, speaking can be incredibly rewarding. As you develop your speaking skills and refine your topics, you can command higher engagement fees. Speaking engagements can lead to other revenue streams, such as workshops, books, online courses, and consulting services. It's a way to diversify your income while doing something you love.

But, as exciting as it can be, speaking is not for everyone. For starters, if you don't naturally enjoy the spotlight or public speaking, the idea of standing in front of an audience can be daunting. The pressure to perform and engage can be overwhelming, and not everyone thrives under such scrutiny.

The life of a professional speaker involves constant travel, irregular schedules, and continually marketing yourself. It all can feel like way too much to deal with. There was a point where I was exhausted just thinking about my next flight. The "glamorous" (sarcasm font) speaker life may not be for you, especially if you value routine or have significant personal commitments.

Financial stability is another consideration. Building a lucrative speaking career takes time, effort, and persistence. It's not a get-rich-quick path, and there may be periods of financial uncertainty, especially in the early stages.

Don't underestimate the emotional toll either. Trolls on the internet can be devastating, but they can be even more hurtful in person. Unfortunately, handling criticism and public scrutiny is part of the job. Not every speech will be well received, and learning to deal with negative feedback constructively is crucial.

Despite all of this, I love being a professional speaker—so much so that I wrote this book to help you become one. If you're passionate about sharing knowledge, influencing change, and connecting with people on a meaningful level, becoming a professional speaker can be incredibly rewarding. It's about making a difference, one speech at a time. However, weighing the challenges and considering whether this career aligns with your strengths and lifestyle preferences is important.

So, give it some thought, now and as you continue to explore the topics in this book. Whether you're ready to take your place on the stage or you're still unsure if this is the path for you, this book will provide the insights you need. Let's explore together what it means to be a professional speaker, helping you make an informed decision about the next steps on your journey.

How This Book Will Help You

The purpose of this book is to help entrepreneurs and executives become radically authentic professional speakers who can deliver a compelling Radical Spark Signature Talk™ from the stage to an engaged audience. My definition of a professional speaker is a performance artist who makes money by clearly communicating helpful ideas from the stage. You are on a stage and performing, hence the "performance artist" part. A performance artist is very different from a boring speaker reading a blog post to an audience. Professional speakers draw their audience in. They make it worth no longer being in your pajamas, having to put on pants and sit your butt in the seat.

The difference between a professional and a hobbyist is money. Professional speakers make money from speaking. When you clearly communicate helpful ideas from the stage, you are being of service and should be compensated for it.

The specific approach to being a professional speaker we are digging into is something I've dubbed "Radically Authentic

Strategic Storytelling™." I like to call it RASS for short because it sounds cool. In relation to being a professional speaker, RASS is the practice of crafting and delivering narratives that are deeply true to the speaker's own experiences, values, and insights while being meticulously designed to achieve specific strategic goals. This approach combines authenticity—speaking from the heart and staying true to yourself—with a strategic framework that ensures the storytelling effectively resonates with, influences, and engages the audience. It empowers speakers to share their unique stories and connect on a profound level, driving meaningful action and fostering genuine relationships. An additional strategic element is how to use speaking to further your larger goals, like getting more clients, gaining visibility, or generating revenue.

Speakers who use Radically Authentic Strategic Storytelling™ are more compelling on stage and can more easily use speaking to make money, whether the organizer pays or not. This book will help you excavate what is no longer serving you, get in touch with your Radically Authentic Self, understand the value in your stories, and help you confidently tell those stories in front of an engaged audience. By the time you have completed reading this book, you will be ready to begin your journey to becoming a professional speaker.

Once I approached being a professional speaker from a place of radical authenticity, my testimonials improved and became more heartfelt. I experienced more referral bookings and was able to increase my rates. The teachings and tools in this book are exactly what I did to become an award-winning international speaker who commands five figures per speaking engagement.

What I am telling you to do in this book works because it has worked for me and my students in my speaker training program, Spark the Stage™. This book will work for you if you do the work.

Just reading the book and nodding in agreement won't get you on stage. I encourage you to use this book as a practical guide. Read each chapter and then put it into practice to see results. You deserve for your speaking career to be more than just something you do "someday."

Already a professional speaker? Don't worry; you are still in the right place. This book will help you create and present more engaging and compelling talks that effectively transform hearts and minds. If you've been looking for ways to stand out from your peers on the speaking circuit, you just found it. Differentiation lies in authenticity.

Our Journey to Getting You on Stage

It is not lost on me that this is a different approach to being a professional speaker than what you might have expected. Most speaker trainers give you a cookie-cutter format or a list of dos and don'ts. I haven't seen that approach create profound, differentiated speakers. Just like I already had all I needed to be successful inside me, you already have a unique and engaging speaker brand inside of you. We just need to excavate it and give you some tools to step out into the glow of your own light.

To get you stage ready, we are going to move through three phases. We are going to get real, get clear, and get connected.

Get Real

In the first section, "Get Real," I invite you to join me for some storytelling, a bit of tough love, and tangible tools to excavate your Radically Authentic Self. The first part of this book will require you to be honest, vulnerable, and courageous. You will take a good look at yourself, what is working, and what is not. By the time you are done reading and participating in the first section, you will have a myriad of tools to connect with your Radically Authentic Self and hear its guidance.

Each short chapter includes an "Essence Expedition." Essence Expeditions are exercises designed to help you get real. The chapters are sequentially ordered to move you from deep excavation of the things holding you back through to replenishment. Essence Expeditions are adventurous explorations into the depths of your true self, which aligns perfectly with uncovering and sharing your authentic stories. I chose the term "Expeditions" to convey the challenge and the excitement of this journey, making it an inviting and intriguing proposition as you complete your quest to find and express your essence on stage. The Essence Expeditions and next steps called Spark Steps may require you to write your thoughts. I suggest you purchase a journal dedicated to your experience with this book.

As you go through the Essence Expeditions, you will also be combating the limiting beliefs that rob you of your confidence. Fear, doubt, imposter syndrome, resentment… all will begin to take a back seat or leave entirely as you move through this process. Although you have an interest in stepping onto the stage, hence why you are reading this book, I also know that most people fear public speaking, and some even fear it more than death. Instead of trying to wrestle the fear to submission, we are going to let it slip to the side as your Radically Authentic Self takes center stage.

The Get Real section of this book is heavy on the "woo." If you haven't picked it up by now, I am a very spiritually inclined person. It is the key to my success. Even my astrologer told me my birth chart could be summed up as the profile of a "business pastor." I don't know how to do business and make money without tapping into Spirit and helping others do the same. The goal is to open you to the beautiful experience of channeling a message to an audience.

If this is not your jam, or you are unsure if this kind of thing is for you, I invite you to try it. Nothing terrible is going to happen to you. It's just a book (and no, it's not the Necronomicon or the Sanderson sisters' book from *Hocus Pocus*). I am not trying to evangelize a particular culture or cult's message or convert you to any religion. The tools I use are based on universal truths found across time, texts, and human experience. As with any tool, if the ones I provide work for you, use them. If they don't work for you, ditch them. The goal is not to become proficient at the tool but to become proficient on stage, using the tools to get there. There are 12 Essence Expeditions in this book. If even one helps you become a more radically authentic speaker, buying this book was money well spent.

Now is probably a good time to talk about certain spiritual words I use in this book. I say things like Spirit, Radically Authentic Self, Source, Universe, God, and Higher Self interchangeably. For me, they all mean the same thing. I am talking about the grander energy that connects us all in love with ourselves and each other. If any of those words make you uncomfortable or you prefer one over the other, just scratch out the word you don't like and replace it with the one you do. I don't care if that word is "the great donut maker in the sky." Do you, boo.

Get Clear

After we riffle around inside of you and help you become a clear channel for your Radically Authentic Self, in the second section called "Get Clear," I will explain how to encapsulate all of your awesomeness so other people can understand it. If you can't clearly articulate the problem you solve for your ideal audience member/client, how you solve it better than anyone else, and what their life looks like after you solve it, all the radical authenticity in the world won't get people to pay attention to you. The best speaker is the clearest speaker.

In this section, I will walk you through, step by step, how to use storytelling frameworks to articulate your message clearly. I will also introduce you to my Crisis Story Framework™, which will help you take your trials and pain and transform them into inspirational messages that will uplift and inspire your audience. Whether you want to be a motivational speaker or you want to speak about a technical subject without your audience falling asleep, storytelling is key to helping your audience understand and take action on the information you provide.

In a world filled with curated personas, authenticity stands out. Sharing genuine stories, with all their imperfections and vulnerabilities, makes you relatable. It shows your audience that you're human, just like them. This authenticity fosters trust and a stronger connection, making your message more impactful.

Mastering the art of storytelling in public speaking isn't just about narrating events; it's about weaving a narrative that touches hearts, triggers emotions, and fosters a genuine connection with your audience. Making your story intersect with theirs transforms your presentation from a simple speech to a memorable experience.

Once you understand how to tell stories and why you are telling them, I will show you how to put them into a Radical Spark Signature Talk™ that keeps an audience engaged from start to finish. I will give you my Radical Spark Signature Talk™ outline framework and advise you on how to create the best slide presentations to accompany your talk.

By the time you are done with this section, you will have everything you need to begin to go out into the world to connect audiences with your message.

Get Connected

Then, it will be time to move forward to how to work the stage and develop a strong stage presence. I'll go over macro concepts like how to project on-stage confidence and micro concepts like what to do with your hands. You will have tangible tools to stand in your power in the spotlight.

After this, if you are like my Spark the Stage™ students, you will be chomping at the bit to get on your next stage. I will give you step-by-step instructions on booking gigs and getting paid for them so you can show off everything you learned in this book. Whether the organizer pays a fee or not, I will give you strategies to make that moolah.

After this section, you will be ready to be a radically authentic professional speaker.

What I Get Out of Writing This Book

I love hearing my fellow authors say, "I just had a book in me that I had to write."

Unfortunately, that is not my story. I didn't have a bunch of spare time on my hands or a sudden urge to see my name on a cover. In fact, this book was written in all of the 'tween times—on planes, via voice recordings while I was walking with my daughter, and in the middle of the night when I had insomnia. I carved out every spare second to ensure this book could exist. Why? Because I wanted to create something to flip the script on how thought leaders craft presentations—not just tweaking the old ways but tossing them out to make room for something fresh and compelling.

I want to help you break free from the moldy molds of presentation-making. I'm here to show you a better way that doesn't just adjust the existing methods but completely revolutionizes the way we think about and create presentations. Let's remove the dusty methodologies from the conversation altogether and start from a place that begins with your unique story.

By breaking away from conventional presentation processes, this book empowers you to avoid becoming another cliché on the speaking circuit. The world doesn't need more speakers who simply tick boxes and deliver forgettable messages. Instead, it craves speakers who can deliver fresh, engaging, and authentically resonant presentations.

Adopting a radically authentic approach means capturing attention and making a memorable impact. This book teaches you how to craft talks that reflect your unique experiences and passions—talks that resonate deeply with the humans in the audience because they arise from genuine insight and personal truth. It's about transforming from a good speaker to an unforgettable one, setting a new standard that celebrates individuality and fosters genuine connections.

Everyone has a story, and I'm passionate about giving you the tools and confidence to tell yours. This book is about transforming nervous speakers into narrative ninjas who can captivate an audience with their authenticity and insights.

Now, before you think I just wrote this book to change the speaking world, I have to come clean. I have a couple of more selfish motivations. Part of the reason I wrote this book is to promote my speaking style—because, let's face it, I want to get booked even more as a keynote speaker. By sharing my approach and philosophy with a broader audience, I'm not just opening doors for more speaking engagements but also hoping to connect with people who resonate with my message. The more I spread the word, the more opportunities I have to step on stages across the globe and share the transformative power of Radically Authentic Strategic Storytelling™. I want to fill my calendar and create a ripple effect of empowerment and inspiration wherever I go.

Shameless plug: If you are an event organizer looking for an engaging speaker to edutain your audience with the power of Radically Authentic Strategic Storytelling™, I would love to chat with you. Please schedule a call at www.aleyaharris.com.

My second slightly selfish motivation is to spread the word about the type of speaking I teach, which brings us to Spark the Stage™. Spark the Stage™ is my online course that helps entrepreneurs and executives become radically authentic professional speakers who can deliver a compelling Radical Spark Signature Talk™ from the stage. The course is this book brought to life with direct access to me in all of my Zoom-filter glory. A smart move would be to read this book and then join the course to get your specific questions answered, participate in a community, and be confident that you are on the right track.

If you want to elevate your speaking game and maybe even revolutionize your career, you'll want to check out Spark the Stage™ at www.aleyaharris.com/spark.

Once again, in writing this book, my goal was to share knowledge and ignite a transformation in how we approach public speaking. This journey through the pages is about giving you the tools to improve your speaking skills and revolutionize them. It's about moving away from outdated norms and embracing a method that starts with your individuality and authentic voice. By the end of this book, I hope to leave you informed and inspired, ready to take the stage by storm and share your unique story in a way that only you can.

The words gracing your eyes right now are part of a manifesto for change in the speaking world, crafted during stolen moments of clarity and bursts of inspiration. I aim to empower you to become a beacon of new-age speaking, someone who brings fresh perspectives and heartfelt stories to light. Let's start this journey together and redefine what it means to be a memorable speaker in today's world.

Let's Take This Conversation Online

I have so many resources to help you become a radically authentic professional speaker that would not fit inside this book. That's why I created an online complement called the Spark Box to give you a more complete experience. The Spark Box includes videos, book recommendations, meditations, and other tools to help you maximize what you learn here. The best part? It is 100 percent free. All you need to access it is your email address.

To access the Spark Box, go to www.aleyaharris.com/spark-box.

I have also included reminders at the ends of certain sections of specific tools in the Spark Box so you don't forget.

Next Steps After Reading This Book

I know you haven't even started getting into the meat of the book yet, but I wanted to suggest a roadmap so your path forward is crystal clear.

1. Read this book and do the Essence Expeditions and Spark Steps. Make sure to use the Spark Box to soak up all of the goodness at www.aleyaharris.com/spark-box.

2. Enroll in Spark the Stage™ at www.aleyaharris.com/spark to review the concepts, connect with the community, and get

feedback. Trying to become a professional speaker in isolation is challenging. The biggest question folks have is, "Am I doing it right?" When you join Spark the Stage™, you will answer that question and feel more confident in your presentation materials and your abilities to captivate an audience.

3. Practice Your New Skills. Start small if you need to. Use these opportunities to practice the techniques you've learned, whether it's a team meeting, a community event, or even a virtual gathering. Every audience interaction is a chance to refine your skills and grow your confidence.

4. Seek Feedback. After your presentations, gather feedback from trusted peers, mentors, or audience members. Constructive feedback is a goldmine for speakers looking to improve. Consider recording your speeches to self-review and determine areas for improvement.

5. Refer Me for Speaking Engagements. If you found value in this book and believe others could benefit from hearing me speak, please refer me to event organizers in your network. Your referrals are precious and help extend the reach of Radically Authentic Strategic Storytelling™. You can send them my website, www.aleyaharris.com, and encourage them to schedule a call.

6. Write a Review. If you loved this book and found it helpful, consider leaving a review on the platform you bought it. Sharing your thoughts helps others discover the book and gain the same valuable insights you did.

Now that we've laid the groundwork and you understand why this book exists and how it can help you, it's time to dive into the heart of our journey together. We start with the "Get Real" section, which is all about peeling back the layers and uncovering the core of your authentic self. Your journey to the stage isn't just about learning to speak well—it's about discovering what makes your voice uniquely powerful and how to harness that power on stage.

In "Get Real," we'll explore why genuine authenticity is your greatest asset as a speaker and how you can cultivate it. This section challenges you to confront and shed the pretenses that hold you back, encouraging you to confidently step into your truth. Through a series of thought-provoking exercises and personal reflections, you'll uncover the real you—the person who doesn't just deliver a message but who resonates with every word they say.

Prepare to delve deep, question your assumptions, and maybe even surprise yourself. So, take a deep breath, and let's begin uncovering the vibrant, genuine speaker within you.

Let's get real.

Section 1
Get Real

"The cave you fear to enter holds the treasure you seek."
—Joseph Campbell

Excavate your authentic self to channel the highest version of you for compelling, transformative public speaking. Through a series of Essence Expeditions and personal stories, this section guides you in shedding outdated narratives and replenishing your spirit, enabling you to connect deeply and resonate with your audience.

This section aims to open you up as a channel because that's what any good performance artist or professional speaker is—a channel. In it, we will focus on the "radically authentic" part of Radically Authentic Strategic Storytelling™. PowerPoint best practices and body language basics are irrelevant if you can't tell a compelling message, and this journey is not just about refining your public speaking skills; it's about excavating the depths of your persona and replenishing your spirit to emerge as a speaker who resonates with truth and connects deeply with every audience.

One of the things that people always say to me when I get off the stage is, "I love your energy!" I always believed it was *my* energy until I had an eye-opening experience one presentation day.

That morning, I was bawling my eyes out in my hotel room. But I had to go on stage. So, I put on my makeup and my fancy dress. I did my hair and put on a happy face as I strutted to the conference area. The whole time, I felt horrible because I was in the pit of postpartum depression and anxiety. I didn't even know which way was up.

I did my presentation, and when I got off stage, people said, "I love your energy!"

That was the moment I knew it wasn't my energy. That was when I realized professional, compelling, radically authentic speakers act as channels for Spirit (or whatever you would like to call your higher power, even if it is your highest version of yourself). Channeling takes the pressure off me to be perfect. Channeling removes the burden of audience transformation from my shoulders. Channeling is the easy route. All you have to do is be open, listen, and follow.

To be an effective channel, you must understand how to open yourself while remaining protected. You need to be open to hearing what your audience needs at that moment. For that reason, I keep my slides super simple to allow the flow of the room to be what it needs to be to get the best result.

My best presentations are the ones where I am prepared, open, and willing to follow. They are the ones where people come up to me afterward in tears, saying how I was able to unlock an "ah-ha" moment. They are the ones where I am genuinely of service.

Before you can effectively channel, you need to get rid of what is no longer serving you. Imagine you are a bucket filled with hot, week-old rancid oyster juice. The stench is overwhelming, turning away anyone who comes near. The bucket symbolizes the negative, stagnant aspects of your past experiences and beliefs that you carry around. These might be old grudges, outdated self-images, or long-held fears that cloud your perception and hinder your effectiveness as a speaker.

Now, imagine yourself wanting to improve or "sweeten" this unpleasant situation by adding something delightful like rich Mexican hot chocolate, infused with its comforting warmth and the spice of cinnamon. Pouring hot chocolate into the rancid oyster juice might seem like a good idea. However, all you achieve is a mixture that's even more repellant than before.

The lesson here is clear: You cannot simply cover up or mask your unresolved issues and negative residues with positive experiences or superficial improvements. To truly transform, you must first empty the bucket of all the old, spoiled contents. This represents the excavation process, where you actively remove those elements in your life that no longer serve you, making room for new, positive experiences.

Once the bucket is clean and empty, you can fill it with something entirely fresh and delightful—like that aromatic Mexican hot chocolate. That Mexican hot chocolate represents replenishment, where you introduce new beliefs, habits, and attitudes that nourish your soul and enhance your ability to connect authentically with your audience.

To truly engage and inspire as a speaker, you must first empty your bucket and refill it with fresh, invigorating content that reflects your true self. This process of excavation and replenishment is essential for anyone stepping onto the stage, as it allows you to present not just with skill but with soul.

Throughout my journey, I've explored various paths of excavation and replenishment, including transformative experiences with Ayahuasca, Insight Seminars, and therapy. Each of these has contributed to my understanding and practice of self-realization, and they complement the exercises we will explore in this book. I designed the following Essence Expeditions to help you excavate, replenish, and become an open channel so you can flourish as a highly potent speaker. They offer you practical, daily steps toward personal authenticity.

It's important to remember: don't get overly attached to the tools themselves. Instead, focus on the feeling of relief and clarity they bring. This emotional resonance will ultimately enhance your speaking engagements and connection with your audience.

As we proceed, you'll encounter various Essence Expeditions and stories that exemplify these concepts. I crafted each chapter to stand alone, allowing you to either progress from one to the following daily or to immerse yourself fully and then revisit specific exercises that resonate with your needs. These stories and exercises are your map to rediscovering and articulating your authentic self, making each speaking opportunity not just a performance but a genuine act of sharing your unique perspective and insights.

Prepare to open yourself up, listen deeply, and allow your true voice to emerge through the art of Radically Authentic Strategic Storytelling™. Your experience in the Essence Expeditions is not just about speaking well—it's about transforming how you see yourself and ensuring your message reaches and profoundly touches your audience. Let's embark on this journey together and unlock the powerful speaker within you.

CHAPTER 1

Take Control of Your Ego

"To thine own self be true."
—Shakespeare's Hamlet, Act I, Scene 3, Polonius

Your ego will prevent you from using vulnerability to connect with yourself and your audience. If you hide behind your ego, your presentations will fall flat.

In December 2022, I was in a daunting financial crisis, buried under a mountain of debt that amounted to nearly $180,000. I was trapped in a financial pit, which only got more treacherous the bigger my ego got.

This is the story of how my ego made me broke.

A year before I finally ended my financial bleeding, I decided to take out a second $30,000 loan in a desperate attempt to keep my business afloat. That brought my total debt to about $60,000. I was accustomed to bringing in $40,000 in monthly revenue, and I needed a quick fix to cover payroll. No big deal, right? However, what began as a temporary slump, justified by my previous successes and the usual ebbs and flows of business revenue, morphed into a relentless rut.

I took out more loans to save my business. Each loan, each financial decision, was a step further into chaos, guided by an ego that whispered reassurances of quick recovery. Taking out loans in my personal name for business expenses should have been my wake-up call, a moment of stark realization that I was veering off course, yet my ego pushed me further into denial.

The descent into financial despair was more than a series of poor decisions; it was a journey marked by overwhelming fear, crushing embarrassment, and a deep-seated sense of guilt. Why didn't I stop sooner? How did I become such a big failure? How was I going to make money?

To top it all off, my daughter, Ruby Coral, was born in November 2022. The emotional turmoil was palpable—I was scared, not just for the future of my business, but for the well-being of my newborn child.

By December 2022, I finally said, "Enough!" I let go of my team and began to lick my wounds. The weight of nearly $180,000 in debt was a constant companion, a reminder of my failures and missteps. The sadness of potentially losing everything I had worked so hard to build was matched only by the guilt of leading myself and my family into this predicament. Amidst the financial chaos, my ego kept me from the truth I needed to confront: I was lost, drowning in a sea of debt, with no apparent way out.

This crisis wasn't just about money; it was a profound personal struggle against the part of me that refused to see reason and clung to false hopes and illusions of control. My journey through financial ruin was a stark lesson in humility and the dangers of letting ego dictate your path. It was a painful realization that sometimes, strength lies in admitting vulnerability, acknowledging that we don't have all the answers, and in opening ourselves to the help and support of others.

The crucial first step in my journey back from the brink was confronting a hard truth—I didn't have all the answers. It was a humbling realization, especially for someone who had built their identity around being a knowledgeable entrepreneur. It was a moment of profound vulnerability, admitting that my expertise had limits and that my ego had blinded me to those limitations.

Acknowledging my ignorance opened the door to seeking help, a move my ego had previously prevented. I turned to America's Small Business Development Center, a decision that proved to be a lifeline. They connected me with advisors who offered practical financial advice and a sense of hope and direction. One advisor, Sebastian DeVivo, helped me see my situation with new clarity and provided actionable steps to address my mounting debt. He connected me with David Desai-Ramierez from AltCap California, a Community Development Financial Institution (CDFI), who helped me escape the grip of predatory loans and find my path to financial recovery. This process of seeking help was transformative, allowing me to leverage expertise beyond my own and start the financial restructuring process.

Perhaps the most challenging step was to share my story openly and honestly, not just with advisors but also with the people I owed money to. This act of transparency was fraught with fear—of judgment, rejection, and further failure. Yet, this very vulnerability began to rebuild the trust I had eroded, and I built solid connections. By being candid about my situation, I could negotiate more manageable repayment terms and, crucially, begin to mend the relationships damaged by my previous decisions.

Each of these steps was a departure from my previous way of doing things, guided by an ego that valued appearance over authenticity and stubbornness over adaptation. By admitting my ignorance, seeking help, and sharing my story, I started to dismantle the ego-driven barriers I had built around myself. This journey was not just about recovering from debt; it was about rediscovering my true self beyond the façade of the all-knowing entrepreneur. It was a lesson in the power of vulnerability, a testament to the strength of admitting our weaknesses, and a rebirth into a more authentic, connected way of being in the world and on the stage.

The path through my financial crisis illuminated a vital truth about vulnerability and its power in public speaking. Just as my ego's drive for self-preservation had obscured my ability to seek help and admit failure, it threatened to sterilize my ability to connect authentically with an audience. The journey taught me that the essence of compelling speaking lies not in perfection or an unattainable veneer of success but in the raw, relatable stories of our struggles and triumphs.

As speakers, embracing our vulnerabilities doesn't weaken our message; it enriches it, making our words resonate on a deeper level. Our audiences don't seek flawless robots on stage; they crave real, flawed humans with whom they can identify and draw strength and inspiration. While fraught with pain and embarrassment, my ordeal became a cornerstone of my speaking philosophy: genuine connection arises not from the stories we think people want to hear but from the genuine narratives of our lived experiences.

This journey taught me the power of vulnerability and the danger of letting ego drive your decisions. As speakers, our goal is to connect authentically with our audience. Hiding behind an ego can prevent that connection, making our presentations fall flat. By taking control of our ego, we open ourselves to genuine engagement, allowing our true selves to shine through and inspire others. This story, a testament to overcoming adversity through authenticity, aligns perfectly with the essence of our first Essence Expedition: taking control of your ego.

Essence Expedition: Take Control of Your Ego

The ego's role is complex. It acts as a protector, seeking to keep us safe and maintain our self-esteem, but it can also become overactive and drive us into decisions that are not aligned with our authentic selves. The ego helps by motivating us and defending our sense of identity, yet it can harm us by pushing us towards inauthentic actions, resisting vulnerability, and limiting our growth.

Taking control of our egos is crucial for speakers because authentic connection with an audience requires vulnerability and openness. By managing our egos, we can present our true selves, fostering genuine engagement and inspiring our listeners.

My friend Monica Laskay introduced me to the strategy of verbally telling my ego who is boss. She encouraged me to read a passage similar to the one below when my ego was wreaking havoc on my body, mind, and emotions. Reading it helped me come into greater balance. I offer my adaptation to help you step into a more vulnerable place, where the power of your Radically Authentic Self lives.

Read the following aloud at least three times. Feel free to add this practice to your daily morning routine.

The ego does not have permission to assume any kind of position, whether I am conscious or unconscious of its actions. The ego no longer has the authority, permission, allowance, freedom, liberty, indulgence, authorization, freehand, or license to make me sick or attached to the past. It does not have permission to push or pull my body out of alignment. The ego only has permission to support me in unconditional loving.

The ego no longer has the authority to judge anything or anyone, including me. It no longer has permission to force me into hiding or fear. It no longer has permission to run exercises of shame and humiliation against me to justify its position. The ego is no longer allowed to hold its own agendas or secrets.

The ego and I no longer need, want, or create separation. The ego no longer needs to avoid money, abundance, or taking care of me. It does not need to deny what is present, avoid making decisions, or limit my freedom. The ego no longer has free reign in my domain.

I accept and acknowledge my responsibility for my creation on all levels. My inner state of being and ego are my creations, and they are not in charge. The authority in me is loving. I choose loving in each situation and circumstance.

Our egos, while intending to protect us, often hinder our connection with ourselves and our audiences. By confronting and controlling our egos, we unlock the ability to share our stories with vulnerability and authenticity, which is essential for compelling speaking. Embracing our genuine selves enhances our presentations and transforms speaking into a powerful tool for connection and change. The strength of your speech lies not in the perfection of your persona but in the authenticity of your narrative.

Spark Steps

- Read the Take Control of Your Ego passage aloud. Consider incorporating it into your morning routine to keep your channel clear and your ego in check.
- If you are looking for free support in your business, contact your local Small Business Development Center (SBDC) by visiting https://americassbdc.org.

- If you are looking for business funding, consider exploring a community development financial institution (CDFI) like AltCap California, the one I had the pleasure of working with.
- Journal Prompts
  - Where has my ego thrown me off track?
  - Write the following in your journal and continue the statement. "Wouldn't it be nice if my ego wasn't in charge? I would…"
- Check out the Spark Box at www.aleyaharris.com/spark-box to grab a free recording of me reading the Take Control of Your Ego passage. Play it as you read along to amplify your efforts.

CHAPTER 2
Forgiveness & Light

"Resentment is like drinking poison and waiting for the other person to die."
—Saint Augustine.

Forgiveness is the antidote. If you are sick, you can't help people into better versions of themselves from the stage.

I walked in, and there she was, hanging. I almost fell backward. I had seen her many times before, but I knew seeing her now meant my night would be much more difficult than I had previously thought. I was about to go deep.

Everywhere my dad moved, he had brought her with him— *Gala Nude Abraham Lincoln* by Salvador Dali. That pasty naked woman was his longest relationship, including the one he had with me. That painting was inextricably linked to my memories of my father, in his glory and pain.

And there she was, taking up most of the wall in the room we were gathering for an Ayahuasca ceremony. Seeing that painting was the Universe's way of telling me tonight was going to be about my daddy issues.

Before I took my first sip of the medicine, I was already nauseous. My stomach was swirling with the poison I had created from my resentful feelings toward my father. Unworthiness, hatred, yearning, grief, abandonment, illusions of freedom, unrequited love, more questions than answers, the contrast between the father I imagined and the reality of the one I have… It was a potent brew.

Soon after the ceremony started, I found the little girl inside me sitting alone in a familiar living room. There was no furniture, only darkness and sadness. I knew I was in one of my father's many homes, in which he promised love but only provided further rejection.

I heard the Spirit of Ayahuasca say, "What do you know for sure?"

My response was, "He's never coming to get me."

Little Aleya had been sitting in that room for years, waiting for the father of her dreams to magically appear, scoop her up into his arms, and tell her that he saw her, that she was worthy and perfect, and that he would put her first. At that moment, I realized he wasn't coming, and it was up to me to get off the floor and leave that room.

Big Aleya abruptly sat up, and my whole body cried away the poison as little Aleya bravely stood up on her small but strong legs, found the exit, and walked away from her prison, never to return. I cried so much I began to convulse. Under the surrealist gaze of Abraham Lincoln and Gala's indifferent back, my husband held me as I purged with tears until I found myself in a healing sleep.

That was the beginning of my forgiveness journey.

To keep from reinjuring myself with resentment, I began to practice the Forgiveness and Light Essence Expedition daily, which I will show you in this chapter. The more forgiveness I employed, the lighter I felt. My creativity opened. My self-esteem increased. I could finally comprehend what it meant to feel whole, worthy, and deeply loved.

I can be vulnerable in this book and on the stage because I've entered into the darkness, rooted it out, and realized that I have nothing to fear. That confidence is palpable when I am on stage. Vulnerability builds connection, helps people feel less alone, and allows us to go on our hero's journeys unencumbered.

The connection between forgiveness and speaking lies in the power of authenticity and emotional liberation. When speakers forgive, they release themselves from the chains of resentment and pain, allowing for a more genuine, heartfelt connection with their audience. A speaker who has embraced forgiveness emanates a sense of peace and openness, inviting the audience into a space of trust and vulnerability.

This Essence Expedition starts off with the person who is often the hardest to forgive: ourselves. Our judgments of our actions, reactions, relationships, and environment usually cause the most damage. As you move through this forgiveness journey, be sure to give yourself grace. Remember, you are divine.

Essence Expedition: Forgiveness & Light

Most of us feel we have to do it, know it, and control it to be safe. We blame others for our circumstances and then grow resentful because they don't do what we want.

Remember, you are an asset. When you squander yourself through resentment, you stay misaligned with your Higher Self. When you use the fullness of your talents to serve, money and opportunities will come to you more readily.

Allow room for vulnerability and accountability because that is where upward movement and change happen. Plant your seeds in fertile ground and trust them to grow.

To release yourself from resentment, I recommend doing the following Essence Expedition at least weekly.

1. Choose your favorite candle (one that you could be close to the smell for at least 15 minutes).

2. Light the candle and place it on the desk or table in front of you.

3. Ask for the Light, the highest purest form of Light, to surround, fill, and protect you for the highest good.

4. Speak forgiveness into the candle. Start with "I forgive myself for judging myself." Afterward, you may say things like, "I forgive my father, and I forgive myself for judging my father." You could also say, "I forgive my body, and I forgive myself for judging my body." Say aloud everything that comes to mind, especially the things you aren't "supposed" to say. This is your time to release.

When you feel complete, end by saying, "I forgive myself for forgetting that I am divine."

Close your eyes and sit in stillness for a moment. You should feel like a weight has been lifted. Revel in the peace.

Forgiveness is the antidote for personal liberation and a vital tool for impactful speaking. By embracing forgiveness, we unlock a profound transformation within ourselves and our ability to connect deeply with others, especially as speakers. The essence of compelling communication lies in our ability to forgive and shed the burdens that mute our authentic voices. Embracing forgiveness allows speakers to connect more deeply, share more openly, and inspire more profoundly, transforming both the speaker and the listener.

This Essence Expedition into forgiveness liberates us from the burdens of resentment and illuminates our path with clarity, enhancing our creativity, self-esteem, and sense of wholeness. As you continue on your journey, remember that forgiving, particularly forgiving ourselves, is a powerful testament to our divinity and resilience. Let this chapter serve as a beacon, guiding you towards embracing vulnerability and authenticity on stage, thereby forging genuine connections and inspiring your audience with your story's truth and light.

Spark Steps

- Decide to forgive.
- Practice Forgiveness & Light. Do it at least weekly to keep yourself clear.
- Need support with this or any of the Essence Expeditions? Email spark@aleyaharris.com with what you need, and my team and I will be there for you.
- Journal Prompts
  - Who do I need to forgive, and what for?
  - How would I go about my life differently if I walked in forgiveness and carried no resentment?
  - How would forgiving make me a better speaker?
- Check out the Spark Box at www.aleyaharris.com/spark-box for some of my favorite candle brands that I like to use with this Essence Expedition.

CHAPTER 3

The Voice of Your Subconscious Mind

"As you sow in your subconscious mind, so shall you reap in your body and environment."
—Joseph Murphy, *The Power of Your Subconscious Mind*

Free your subconscious mind from negative thoughts so that you can experience success in life and on the stage.

Once I started the forgiveness journey of releasing my daddy issues, the real work began. The problem was that I didn't know how to move forward because I felt stuck in a narrative told by a petty tyrant in my head. My subconscious mind, despite my pleading to the contrary, was holding onto all of the pain and refused to release it.

The pain had become a safety blanket, the basis of large parts of my identity and the foundation of my excuses. I was scared I wouldn't be able to determine who I was if I let it go. But the wiser part of me also knew that if I held onto the hurt, I would move through life with a ball and chain tied around my ankle, never able to hit my perfect stride.

Luckily, I was introduced to Free Form Writing, the Essence Expedition for this chapter. Free Form Writing is where you intentionally sit down, let your subconscious spout its negativity from a soap box, and then let it go. It makes your subconscious feel heard while shattering the broken record in your head that prevents you from creating new, beautiful music.

I still remember one of my early sessions vividly. I sat down to release negativity around my relationship with my father and confront my fear of doing so. As soon as I put pen to paper, I felt like my hand had a mind of its own. I started to feel heat rising from my stomach to my chest, to my throat, and finally out of my mouth. My hand furiously scribbled as I started panting, growling, grunting, and yelling. The heat moved up to my face, and tears that reflected much more than sadness sprang from my eyes. Every stroke across the page made me feel like I was being rewritten.

I don't know how long I was writing, but I felt exhausted, peaceful, and grateful when I was done. I couldn't even get up from my desk, so I just laid my head down and fell asleep. In my dream, I saw my father. I hugged him and thanked him for the blessings he had given me, even if at the time they felt more like curses. I realized that he completed his karmic role in my life perfectly. His job was to help me explore feeling marginalized, abandoned, and unworthy so that I could develop an intimate knowledge of how to build confidence, clarify my identity, and better serve others on a similar journey. As I experienced that epiphany, I watched him walk into the Light. For the first time, I felt complete even in his absence.

When I woke up, I knew I had created a profound shift. I had taken a large chunk of the pain away and would have a greater ability to stand in my worth and honor myself as a valuable human being. It was a gift for my heart—and surprisingly, my bank account. Soon after, I began to scrutinize my rates. I had been woefully underpricing my time. I stepped into my worthiness and increased the fees for my consulting services by 500 percent. The coolest part? People paid the new prices without batting an eye. At the time of writing this, my consulting rates are 1,316 percent higher than before that amazing Free Form Writing session, and I know I am worth every penny (and so do the clients who gratefully pay me).

I cannot guarantee the same results for you because we are all different. But I can guarantee that when you clear your subconscious mind, you are removing roadblocks to your success, and good things will follow.

Incorporating Free Form Writing into my routine catalyzed my healing and profoundly enhanced my public speaking. By clearing subconscious limitations, I connected more authentically with my audience and enhanced the impact of my words. This authenticity built trust and demonstrated the inherent value of my story, empowering me to recognize and assert my worth.

Recognizing the value of my narrative was crucial, especially as I began to navigate the speaking circuit. While paying your dues is a part of the journey, understanding that your unique insights are worthy of compensation is vital. This realization led me to confidently price my speaking engagements, reflecting the actual value I bring to the stage. As you embark on this exercise, embrace your story's worth and understand that you deserve compensation for your unique contributions through your talks.

Essence Expedition: Free Form Writing

Give your subconscious a voice and clear the exhausting burdens keeping you from letting your genius change the world.

Free Form Writing is different from journaling. You don't read it, it doesn't matter how neat your handwriting is, and you don't stop your hand from moving as you write. After you have finished, you rip up the paper or burn it (safely). This experience is about letting go, not immortalizing our shackles.

1. Set an intention for clearing compassion and creativity blocks before you start writing.

2. Protect your space and calendar.

3. Light a candle. Get a pen/pencil and paper. Remember, you will throw this away, so don't use your cute journal with the linen pages.

4. Allow a thought into your mind and transfer it into the pen. You may not even finish a sentence before the next thought comes up. For example, the thought, "go to the restaurant together," arises. As you start to write "together," you may get T-O-G-E . . . and then the next word or thought that comes up is "help," and you may write H-L-P. That is just fine because you know what you mean by it.

5. When you are done, don't read it. Rip it up, burn it, and let it go. (Be safe while burning it, please!)

Spark Steps

- Decide that feeling good is the most important.
- Practice Free Form Writing. Do it at least weekly to keep yourself clear.
- Journal Prompts

- How have I seen the negative feelings I hold in my subconscious mind affect my life?
- What would my life be like if I only thought positive thoughts and saw their impact on my life?
- Do I believe thinking negative thoughts or feeling negative feelings is necessary? If so, why? If not, then why do I think and feel them?

CHAPTER 4

Clear the Energy

**"What drains your spirit drains your body.
What fuels your spirit fuels your body."**
—Carolyn Myss

You are the energetic sovereign of the empire of you. Keep your empire clean. After all, you have to live there. Plus, speaking is very similar to accounting—garbage in, garbage out. If you don't continue to excavate your empire, you will dump your trash on your audience. That's the opposite of being of service from the stage.

When you get a gross feeling, clear your energy.
When you are around a lot of people, clear your energy.
When you have just gone through an illness, clear your energy.
You can and should clear your energy field multiple times daily to stay connected and channeling.

When I talk about your energy, I mean the energy systems that surround, flow through, and penetrate your body. Even though you don't see microwaves, you know that your Gluten Free Mac & Cheese From Trader Joe's will be piping hot in five minutes. You don't see radio waves either, but you can discern that "Cowboy Carter" by Beyoncé is on full repeat. In much the same way, most people cannot see their energy field, but that doesn't make it any less there.

Your energy can become "sticky" and trap unwanted thoughts, feelings, illness, etc., from others, your own mind, and your environment. All that trash can negatively affect your mindset, physical well-being, and spiritual health. Clearing your energy keeps you squeaky clean and drama free.

As a speaker, part of my job is to keep my energy clear so I can make sure the advice, tools, and engagement I offer are about my audience and that my time on stage is not some grand personal therapy session. Speakers often get confused and think that speaking is all about them because they are the ones with the mic and in the spotlight. It is not. It is about each audience member and how the experience with you can change their life. But, if you schlep all of your energetic baggage onto the stage, you can easily slide into the role of a narcissistic energy vampire who craves attention because it makes them feel better about themself.

It is also essential to clear your energy because the audience is off-gassing many of their issues into the room, often directed at you. They aren't doing it maliciously or even intentionally, but it can still leave you feeling like you've been struck by Miley Cyrus' wrecking ball when you step off the stage. If you are doing your job correctly, you encourage your audience to transform old mindsets, which usually requires them to think about past or current challenges, even briefly. You don't want their challenges to become yours.

Luckily, there are several ways to clear your energy, and I invite you to incorporate them into your daily routine, like your shower, 10-step K-beauty skincare routine, or toothbrushing.

Essence Expedition: Clear the Energy

Energy blockages settle in for the long haul unless you actively clear them out. Severing guilt, resentment, and trauma can unleash new ideas for Radical Spark Signature Talks™, stories to tell from the stage, and ways to leverage speaking to grow your business and career.

Santo & Sage

1. Open a window or door.

2. Set your intention for clearing and invite in the Light.

3. Carefully light green or blue sage and walk around your space, fanning the smoke into the room. If the sage stops smoking, you may need to carry the lighter with you.

4. Snuff the sage in a fire-safe container or let it burn itself out.

5. Repeat with Palo Santo.

Your intentions, thoughts, and feelings are essential in the clearing process. As you move through your space, focus on positivity.

This type of clearing is lovely for the general maintenance of your mental and physical space and spiritual tools.

Salt & Fire

You can also clear your space with Epsom salt and rubbing alcohol by placing a disposable aluminum bowl filled with ¼ cup of Epsom salt and ½ cup of rubbing alcohol on an old cookie sheet (the cookie sheet will not be suitable for baking after this).

1. Open a window or door.

2. Set your intention for clearing and invite in the Light

3. Light the alcohol and Epsom salt on fire and, using oven mitts, walk around your space. Be careful of the flames, as they can get quite high. Continue clearing until the fire burns out.

4. Let the cookie sheet sit on a heat-resistant surface until it cools down.

5. Throw away the aluminum bowl with the Epsom salt outside.

I like to do this and chant Ani-Hu at the same time. You can read more about that Essence Expedition in Chapter Seven: Hey, God. It's me.

This process works well for stubborn energy and thought forms. Thought forms are energetic bundles that you can create when you repeatedly think about a specific topic. A thought form that you generate by obsessing consciously or subconsciously over something negative can block your communication with Spirit and prevent you from being an effective channel. If you have been feeling heavy, sick, stuck, or confused, clearing your energy with salt and fire could be an excellent option.

Brine Bath

Take a bath in Epsom salt to clear your body's energetic field. I find it most critical to do this before and after a large speaking engagement. I do it before to be as present as possible and not put any of my limitations onto the audience. I do it afterward because connecting with many people on and off the stage can cause your energetic field to become misaligned. Plus, you don't know what may transfer from someone to you. Taking a brine bath helps to clear, realign, and reenergize and is especially key for multi-day speaking engagements and conferences.

No bathtub? Rub your moistened body with Epsom salt and rinse off in the shower. This also has the lovely side effect of exfoliation and skin softening (you didn't know you were gonna get beauty tips in this book, did ya?).

Note: Shave *after* you do anything with Epsom salt. Otherwise, it will sting. Yes, I am speaking from personal experience.

Hand to Head

Throughout the day, take your right hand, place it over your forehead, and silently or aloud say, "Clear, disengage, and disconnect through the Light, for the highest good," while you move your fingertips up and down the bridge of your nose. These words declare your intention to separate from the negativity and return to the comfort of your energy field. You are actively clearing your third eye, the seat of your intuition.

If you attend one of my speaking engagements, you may see me doing this often. For me, it is crucial to maintain a clear communication channel with Spirit so I can serve the audience for the highest good. The clearer I am of interfering thoughts, emotions, and beliefs, the better I speak and serve.

Spark Steps

- Incorporate energy clearing into your daily practice.
- Actively clear your energy before and after you are on the stage.
- Journal Prompts

- ○ When I read the word "energy," what is my reaction? Is there resistance, and if so, why?
- ○ This one's for the not-so-woo: How would my behavior change if I believed in energy and its ability to impact my life?
- ○ After you do one or more of the Essence Expeditions from the chapter, write down how you feel.
- Check out the Spark Box at www.aleyaharris.com/spark-box for some of my favorite clearing tools and other resources to help you get more in touch with your Radically Authentic Self.

CHAPTER 5

Versus Battle

"You get more and more of what you are thinking about—whether you want it or not."
—Abraham-Hicks

You should have a clear picture of what strategies and approaches are truly serving your growth as a speaker versus those that are holding you back. By identifying and eliminating ineffective habits, you'll be able to fine-tune your presentation skills and amplify your impact on stage.

Sometimes, the universe whispers to us through our bank accounts; for me, it shouted. Postpartum depression clouded my perception, and financial instability racked me with stress. Yet, amidst this chaos, Abraham-Hicks' teachings became my beacon of hope, guiding me from a world of despair to one where opportunities blossomed effortlessly.

While checking my ego was essential to transcending my situation, it wasn't enough to reverse the deep-seated sadness. I needed to take control of my emotional state, and I had no idea how. Luckily, the Universe had my back. One day, a remarkable woman contacted me on LinkedIn and asked if I wanted to join her manifestation book club. My answer was an immediate "yes."

Our first book was *Ask and It Is Given* by Abraham-Hicks. That book changed my life.

Abraham is a non-physical collective consciousness that is channeled at will by Esther Hicks. *Ask and It is Given* was delivered to Esther in a non-physical form, and much of it is written through Abraham's voice. Although the book is officially written by Esther and Jerry Hicks, I, and others who are familiar with this book series, refer to the author by Abraham-Hicks to touch upon the partnership between the physical and non-physical collaborators.

The core of Abraham-Hicks' teachings is that we are all powerful creators who can craft our realities through focused attention on what we want. We can use our emotions as a guidance system to determine how close to or far we are from manifesting our desires. When we are depressed, we are far away. When we feel love and gratitude, we are in alignment with that which is for our highest good. The overarching concept is that like attracts like, and whatever you focus on in your thoughts and feelings will manifest in your reality.

As a new mother grappling with emotional turmoil and a staggering array of business challenges, I was very far from being in alignment. Each day, I faced the dual pressures of nurturing a newborn and reviving a floundering business. It was during this exhausting dance between diapers and deadlines that I stumbled upon the transformative teachings of Abraham-Hicks.

Despite my openness to "woo," a part of me wondered about the practical effects of such a spiritual approach. Financial pressures were mounting, and my emotional well-being was frayed. The promise of shifting my mindset to manifest my desires was compelling. Could focusing on positivity truly transform my reality so profoundly?

But I figured that I didn't have anything to lose. Being more positive and focusing on feeling good couldn't bring anything bad with it, so I embraced Abraham-Hicks' principles wholeheartedly. Each morning, I replaced my worries with gratitude, focusing on positive visualizations of my day. My new manifestation practice wasn't just a routine; it was a heartfelt alignment that shifted my energy from desperation to hopeful anticipation.

This shift in mindset brought remarkable professional opportunities. One vivid example was when a dear client needed to elevate his business valuation from $2 million to a much higher figure. He emailed me and said he urgently needed my magic. He paid me $5,000 for my work. The best part? Early that week, I visualized receiving an extra $5,000 and using what I had learned from Abraham-Hicks to create my reality. I got paid and crafted a story that repositioned his business, resulting in an astounding reevaluation at $51 million. (Yes, now I charge much more for this service because of the ROI). This was not just a win for my client but a profound validation of my new approach to revenue generation.

The success bred more success. Speaking engagements became more frequent and more fulfilling. Opportunities began to find me. Debts magically were paid off or canceled. I am never turning back from focusing on what is working and letting the Universe handle the rest. It just feels too good.

This journey through the teachings of Abraham-Hicks taught me an invaluable lesson as a professional speaker. When we align our internal narrative with positivity and focus on our desires, we attract opportunities that reflect our optimistic outlook. For speakers, this alignment is crucial—it enhances our connection with the audience and magnifies our impact, turning each engagement into a potentially life-changing encounter.

By applying these lessons, I discovered the true power of mindset in overcoming obstacles and achieving professional success. The universe had spoken, and I had listened with an open heart and a willing spirit, ready to embrace the abundance that awaited.

This chapter's Essence Expedition will help you start you on your journey of knowing what is working in your life and what isn't. Magnify what is working and let go of the rest. Lean into the positive aspects of your life and invite in more abundance.

Essence Expedition: Versus Battle

Feedback is all around you. Landed that deal and feeling good about it? That's feedback. Lost that client, even though you tried your best? That's also feedback. Feedback is neutral. Your reaction to it will determine your emotional state.

Take a step back and observe your life. What is working for you? What is working against you?

In your journal, divide a sheet of paper into two columns. On one side, write what is working for you. On the other side, write what is working against you.

Don't overthink it, and be wary of the word "should." Just because you have one talk doesn't mean you should keep it. Have an ineffective team member that's sweet and has been with you forever? That doesn't mean that things should keep being mediocre. Now's your chance to switch it up.

Don't judge it; just observe. Then, take action. Amplify what works for you and remove what doesn't to leave room for greater abundance.

Spark Steps

- I highly recommend you purchase and read *Ask and It Is Given* by Abraham-Hicks.
- Create a list of what is working and what is not working for you. Lean into the fantastic feeling you get when you focus on what's working.
- Journal Prompts
  - Write about an aspect of your life or work governed by "shoulds'" rather than your genuine desires. What keeps you tied to these "shoulds"? How do they affect your emotional well-being and alignment with your true self?
  - Reflect on a recent day when you felt particularly aligned or misaligned with your emotions. What were the circumstances? Describe the feelings and thoughts that dominated the day.
  - Reflect on a limiting belief that you suspect has been holding you back in your personal or professional life. Describe how this belief has manifested in your actions and decisions. What positive belief could replace this limiting one?

CHAPTER 6

Know When Not to Speak

"Silence is the great teacher and to learn its lessons you must pay attention to it. There is no substitute for the creative inspiration, knowledge, and stability that come from knowing how to contact your core of inner silence."
—Deepak Chopra

Mastering the art of silence is as crucial as mastering the art of speaking. Strategic pauses and choosing your moments wisely can make your message more impactful. Sometimes, the most powerful communication happens without words.

In elementary school, I was the kid who always got in trouble for talking. I just couldn't contain my commentary on the lesson, my feelings, my questions... everything was up for grabs in my frequent side chats with my neighbor (I don't think my neighbors appreciated it very much. I was also working on self-awareness.). I could have gotten away with it, but I didn't know how to whisper. Even if the other person spoke to me first, my response was so loud that I was the one the teacher heard; hence, I was the one who got chastised.

You would think I learned my lesson after this happened many times, but I didn't. Instead, I became a professional speaker so I could talk without having to sit in the corner for 10 minutes to think about what I'd done. As I was beginning my speaking career, I erroneously thought that being a natural chatterbox was going to be my key to success. Actually, it was my ability to sit in silence that made the most significant impact on my stage performance.

I leaned into figuring out how to leverage silence as a speaker while juggling my roles as a new mother and entrepreneur. I found myself overwhelmed by the incessant noise of life. My mind was a cacophony of words around processing my changed world, planning, and pushing forward. It was during this chaotic period that I stumbled upon the idea of a silent retreat—a concept that was as intimidating as it was intriguing for someone like me who thrived on expression.

Despite my reservations, I knew I needed a change. My brain needed quiet (much like my poor seat neighbors in elementary school). I was curious—and desperate enough—to see if silence could bring the serenity I was seeking. I thought about going all in on a three-day silent retreat, but that seemed about as realistic as politely asking my baby not to cry and her acquiescing. Instead, I committed to finding two minutes of silence each day. My goal was to replace my unending internal monologue and external speech with reflection and peace.

In the beginning, silence was really uncomfortable for me. I felt like I should be doing something or saying something. It felt like a waste of time. But as I remained consistent, something remarkable began to happen. Stripped of my usual crutches of constant conversation and connectivity, I was forced to confront the thoughts and feelings I'd been too busy to address. I think these moments of silent reflection were critical in my postpartum healing journey.

It wasn't just the absence of noise that was transformative; it was the quality of presence I found within that silence. I realized that my best work, the moments when I truly connected with my audience, wasn't when I was meticulously sticking to my talking points. It was when I allowed myself to be present and open, channeling the authenticity and inspiration that silence had nurtured.

Now, I practice my silence moments while cuddling Ruby Coral to sleep. I sit with her warm little body in my arms and use her adorable snores as the background track to my gratifying moments of silence. These moments are my favorite each day. They are when I feel the most complete and connected with my Highest Self.

As a speaker, you don't need to fill every moment with words. Allow space for silence in your daily life, and let those quiet moments inform and inspire your speech.

Essence Expedition: Shhh...

Have you ever thought about how much you talk? I don't mean from the stage but in your daily life. If you're an extrovert like me who processes externally, the endless stream of words flowing out of your mouth can be dizzying.

And it's not just you and me blabbing on and on. Everyone does it. Isn't it astounding how noisy our world is? Silence is a rare commodity.

And yet, it is in silence that we find our authentic selves. It is the space between the words, thoughts, and breaths where the magic of creation lives. We just need to be still enough to experience it.

In our calendar-controlled daily routines, finding space for silence can seem impossible. However, I challenge you to prioritize silence daily. It could be for two minutes or two hours. The point is to stop doing and start being. In the being, you will find connection, and in connection, you will find an open channel to your Highest Self.

It's not a herculean task. It is only as complicated as you make it. Go out into nature, if available, and sit in silence. Commune with the peace that exists in between breaths. Stay for a few more moments in the shower and appreciate the feeling of the water on your body. Sit in your car before your next appointment and find stillness. The amount of information that lives in silence is awe-inspiring. When you begin to practice silence regularly, you'll become eager for your next moment of tranquility.

Spark Steps

- Seek, create, and protect moments of silence. Strive to experience silence daily.
- Journal Prompts
  - Reflect on a typical day in your life. How much of it is filled with unnecessary noise, both external (like TV, conversations, and city sounds) and internal (your thoughts and self-talk)? Describe how this noise affects your mood and energy levels.
  - Why do you think silence feels uncomfortable or like a "waste of time" for many people? How could embracing moments of stillness daily transform your perspective on productivity and rest?
  - How can you incorporate daily moments of silence into your routine, like how I find peace while cuddling Ruby

Coral? Plan a simple, daily silence practice and describe how you think it might affect your daily life and your speaking abilities.

CHAPTER 7

Hey, God. It's me.

"Meditation isn't about becoming a different person,
a new person, or even a better person. It's about training in
awareness and understanding how and why you think and
feel the way you do, and getting a healthy sense of perspective
in the process."
—Andy Puddicombe, Headspace co-founder

Active meditation is the biggest "pro tip" I can give you to mastering the stage. By channeling your inner silence through practices like chanting Ani-Hu, you transform your speaking into an authentic act of connection, allowing you to resonate deeply with every audience member. Remember, speaking is like sculpting—the real art lies not just in what you add but in what you remove. Embrace active meditation to clear away the noise and reveal the compelling speaker within you, ensuring you deliver a message and an experience.

I grew to hate Andy. At first, I was excited because his voice was smooth, reassuring, and British. There's just something about a British accent that makes us Americans feel like we are in good hands. At the beginning of our relationship, I was confident that Andy would be the perfect person to guide me into my bliss.

I would sit down daily and listen to Andy's melodious voice in the Headspace app tell me to focus on my breath. I would attempt to clear my mind and just be. I gave myself grace in the beginning. I couldn't focus my mind on anything. Sometimes I would fall asleep. Or I would just let it play and unconsciously ignore Andy and his calming nudges to be present. I was sure with consistent practice, it would get better. It did not.

The more I tried to empty my mind, the more frustrated I got. I grew resentful of Andy's smug colonizer perkiness. This former monk could meditate for up to 16 hours daily, and I struggled with 20 minutes. Every time I clicked on the orange dot to open the meditation app, I felt like a failure. Meditation began to feel like a chore at best and a tool to remind me of my incompetence at worst. It wasn't long before I gave up on meditation, feeling defeated.

Soon after, I became familiar with the Movement of Spiritual Inner Awareness (MSIA) and spiritual exercises, including active meditation using a tone. For me, it was a game changer. The goal switched from trying to empty my mind and focus on my breath to concentrating on something audible. It allowed me to use one of my ingrained talents as a speaker, my burning desire to vocalize, to better connect with myself and Spirit. I could finally experience moments of bliss, receive insights, and manage stress more effectively.

I have since forgiven Andy (it wasn't his fault, really). I just needed to find the tool that best fit me and how I operate. Meditation is not about pumping up your ego and bragging about how good at it you are or how long you can do it. It is about connecting with Spirit and your Radically Authentic Self. As I said in the intro, don't get attached to the tool. Find what works for you to excavate, replenish, and connect to channel effectively.

Now, I teach audiences how to chant Ani-Hu from the stage. It is such a blissful sound to hear hundreds of people chanting at once and then feel the energy in the room shift. For many of them, it is their first time doing active meditation, and I become their Andy, their guide on the journey of self-discovery. I don't even need a British accent. I invite them, just like I invite you, to try active meditation. If it works, awesome. If it doesn't, ditch it and find the tool that works for you to connect.

If you want to hear how Ani-Hu sounds, go to the Spark Box at www.aleyaharris.com/spark-box, where you will find a recording of me chanting. Feel free to chant with me and use the recording to support your active meditation practice.

Incorporating active meditation into my routine profoundly improved my well-being and significantly enhanced my capabilities as a professional speaker. This practice allowed me to harness the same focus and presence I discovered through chanting Ani-Hu and apply it to connect with audiences in a more profound, more meaningful way. As speakers, our goal is not just to convey information but to resonate on a vibrational level with our audience, creating a shared experience that is both enlightening and transformative.

Active meditation, particularly through vocalizations like Ani-Hu, trains you to manage your internal energy and direct it outward in controlled, impactful ways. This skill is invaluable on stage, where maintaining composure, focus, and emotional connection with the audience can make the difference between a forgettable speech and a memorable experience. It teaches you to channel your energy and Spirit effectively, ensuring that every word, pause, and breath is infused with intention and authenticity.

By embracing active meditation, you'll find that your presence as a speaker is not just about what you say but how you say it and the unspoken energy you communicate. This practice helps to dissolve the barriers between speaker and listener, allowing for a flow of energy that captivates and connects. Whether you're guiding a room through a chant or delivering a keynote, your ability to be fully present and connected to your Highest Self will leave a lasting impact on your audience.

So, as you continue to explore and integrate active meditation into your daily routine, remember that this isn't just about personal tranquility—it's a powerful tool in your arsenal as a speaker that enhances your ability to connect, inspire, and lead with radically authentic energy.

Essence Expedition: Active Meditation

If you are like most novice meditators, the idea of emptying your mind is daunting (and you've probably fallen asleep at least once). Instead of creating a mind void, focus on a positive tone. It is much easier, and you will get more tangible results.

My favorite tone to chant is "Ani-Hu" (Sounds like "On-Eye Hue").

Hu is Sanskrit and is an ancient name for God/Spirit/Universe, and the Ani in Ani-Hu brings in the quality of empathy. It is literally like saying, "Hey, God. It's me. I could benefit from you understanding and connecting with me right now." Chanting Hu or Ani-Hu will help clear blockages and open you up for greater awareness and trust. It works best when you do it daily or even multiple times per day. Devout Ani-Hu practitioners strive for two hours per day. I've never quite gotten there, but I imagine it is transcendent.

You can also chant "Om," defined by Hindu scripture as the primordial sound of creation. It is the original vibration of the universe. When chanted, Om vibrates at the frequency of 432 Hz, which is the same vibrational frequency found throughout everything in nature. I first chanted Om on a beach in Mexico during a wellness session at a conference where I was speaking. I instantly felt a buzzing in my belly that intrigued me to continue exploring how this tone could deepen my connection with my Radically Authentic Self.

Regardless of the tone you choose, here are some general guidelines to get the most out of your chanting experience:

1. Sit upright in a quiet place where no kids, dogs, or partners will disturb you. Put your devices on do not disturb or physically move them to a different room.

2. Ask for the Light, the highest purest form of Light, to surround, fill, and protect you for the highest good.

3. Inwardly or outwardly, chant "Ani-Hu" or "Om." While chanting, focus on the dark screen behind your closed eyelids. Allow the movie to develop, and enjoy the show.

4. When you feel complete, stop chanting, give thanks, wash your hands, and drink water. You may feel a tad dizzy, so be mindful and careful.

Spark Steps

- Try active meditation for at least a week. Note how you feel and any insights you have.

- Give yourself grace, and don't take this (or anything) too seriously. There is no celestial judge or proctor who will come down on a cloud and give you a passing or failing grade at meditation. Active meditation is a tool to feel good.
- Journal prompts
  - Answer the following questions in your journal: Why am I so busy? What is it all for? What could I feel like if I had more margin in my life?
  - Coco Chanel said, "Once you've dressed, and before you leave the house, look in the mirror and take at least one thing off." If you applied that thought to your life, what would be the one extra item that you would remove? What would you feel like if you replaced that time with active meditation?
  - What is your relationship with God? For some, even the word makes them uncomfortable. What healing could you experience that would remove your barriers to connection?
- Check out the Spark Box at www.aleyaharris.com/spark-box to download a free recording of me chanting Ani-Hu. You can use it to help focus as you chant along.

CHAPTER 8

Just Breathe

"We need to lead with our feminine—which is intuition, flow and compassion and follow with the masculine energy of execution and action."
—Francesca Sipma, HypnoBreathwork® creator

It is easier to construct a city with a stroll than a sledgehammer. Letting go of hard work and tuning in can lead to more profound connections with your audience and turn your speaking into a powerful, effortless act of sharing your true self. Allow your authentic voice to flow freely and embrace the ease that brings success without the struggle.

I got high on my own supply, and it rocked my world. My client and friend, Diane Lam, had turned me on to HypnoBreathwork® and an app called Mastry. She is always finding great tools to deepen her relationship with her Highest Self, and I figured I could at least do it once to tell her that I did it. I had tried breathwork in the past but hadn't fallen in love with using it as a tool. I had low expectations, but I figured the worst that could happen was that I would fall asleep. I probably needed a good nap anyway.

When I laid down and turned on the app, I prepared myself to have a calming 22.8 minutes of easeful meditation. That's not what happened. I clicked on the "Abundance HypnoBreathwork®"

recording because, well… you've read the book up until this point. You get it. I settled in as Francesca Sipma calmly repeated, "Inhale belly. Inhale chest. Exhale." In rhythm with the surprisingly upbeat music, I spent the first several minutes trying to figure out the awkward breathing pattern. And then, I felt the shift.

Instead of breathing, I was being breathed. I tuned into a vein of pent-up feelings, memories, and power I had never felt outside of an Ayahuasca ceremony. Tears burst from my eyes, my body began to tremble, and what felt like eons of trapped negativity released itself from my body and my Spirit. As the recording continued, I felt more connected and open than I had in a long time. I had finally let go.

At that moment I realized that everything didn't have to be so hard.

Being a success, feeling freedom, reaching my goals… I was pushing so hard that I was my own worst enemy.

After the recording ended, I lay on my back with two ears full of tears and a heart that felt lighter than it had in a long time. I made a note in the app that said, "Thank Diane" as my next step. But the Universe wasn't done with me yet. Soon after, my husband introduced me to the song "Jericho" by Iniko.

Jericho is a Bible story, and yes, I am going to go through the Bible verse to help me illustrate the point that hard work is not the answer. But please do not think that you need to be a believer in any particular religion or spiritual belief or practice; I am not proselytizing or evangelizing. The story that just so happens to come from the Bible is very illustrative of ubiquitous spiritual principles that are within all cultures.

When I heard the song for the first time, I began to remember Jericho falling in a unique way. They didn't beat the thing down with sledgehammers or throw big rocks at it. All they did was walk around it.

I realized that since I have the choice between sledgehammers and walking, between burnout or ease, between struggle or just breathing, I choose the Jericho way. It was exactly the type of effort and spiritual partnership I was looking for. To move forward with my life, to not be so stressed out, and to not continually activate diseases within me that prevent me from reaching my goals, I had to do something differently.

The Bible verse is:

The Lord said to Joshua, "Look, I have handed Jericho, its king, and its fighting men over to you. March around the city with all the men of war, circling the city one time. Do this for six days. Have seven priests carry seven ram's-horn trumpets in front of the ark. But on the seventh day, march around the city seven times, while the priests blow the trumpets. When there is a prolonged blast of the horn and you hear its sound, have all the people give a mighty shout. Then the city wall will collapse, and the people will advance, each man straight ahead." (Joshua 6:2-5 HCSB).

Once I read that verse, it all came together.

1. What I want is already mine.

2. If I follow the leading of Spirit, even if the directions seem a bit odd, I will manifest what I want. I can choose to trust instead of worry. I can partner with Spirit along my journey.

3. I don't have to fight. I can reach my goals with joy and minimal, inspired action.

4. My resistance is the only thing preventing me from getting what I want.

This transformative journey through breathwork and the lessons of Jericho taught me that success in speaking—and in life—doesn't have to be forced; it can flow naturally when aligned with our highest selves and our divine guidance. By adopting the Jericho way, I learned to approach each speaking engagement not as a battle to be won with sheer force but as a space to share, inspire, and connect deeply using the least amount of effort but with the most meaningful impact. I am still a recovering type A+, but I am now on a much better path.

You are already a successful professional speaker. You are just still walking around your walls.

As speakers, we often think the only path to captivating our audience is through relentless preparation and energetic performance. However, my experience showed me that real power lies in simplicity and authenticity. By letting go of the need to control every detail and instead embracing the flow of intuitive guidance, I became more resonant with my audience, my messages became more impactful, and my speaking became more profound. This approach doesn't just reduce stress; it amplifies your ability to connect, transforms your presence on stage, and makes every word you speak a conduit for the energy you wish to share.

This chapter's exploration of breathwork and the metaphorical walls we need to let crumble naturally invites you to rethink how you approach your role as a speaker. Let this be your invitation to shift from doing to being—from pushing to allowing—and to discover how your authentic voice and the power of Spirit can elevate your speaking from good to transformational. Just breathe.

Essence Expedition: Just Breathe

I highly recommend downloading the Mastry App and trying out their tools. I have found them to be transformative. You can go to the Spark Box at www.aleyaharris.com/spark-box to get a free 30-day subscription to Mastry.

Breathwork is a powerful tool for unlocking and releasing trapped emotions. It allows you to connect more deeply with your authentic self and enhance your ability to communicate from the heart. This Essence Expedition will guide you through a simple yet profound breathwork practice designed to release emotional blockages, foster relaxation, and prepare you for more authentic and impactful speaking.

Instructions:

Find a Comfortable Space: Find a quiet, comfortable place to sit or lie down. Ensure you won't be disturbed for the next 10-20 minutes. Use cushions or blankets to support your body if needed.

Set an Intention: Close your eyes and take a few natural breaths. Set an intention for this session. It could be something like, "I release what no longer serves me" or "I open myself to speak from a place of authenticity and ease."

The Breath Pattern:

Part 1: Deep Belly Breathing – Place one hand on your stomach and the other on your chest. Inhale deeply through your nose, directing the air into your belly so it rises while your chest remains relatively still. Feel the hand on your stomach rise, then exhale fully through your mouth, letting your belly fall. Continue this deep belly breathing for about 3 minutes, focusing on filling and emptying your belly.

Part 2: Energizing Breath - Inhale through your nose for a count of 4, hold your breath for a count of 7, then exhale forcefully through your mouth for a count of 8, making a whoosh sound. Repeat this cycle four times. This helps to build energy and prepare the body to release trapped emotions.

Active Release Breathwork:

Continuous Connected Breathing – Now, transition to a rhythmic and continuous breath cycle. Inhale and exhale without pauses through the mouth at a steady, fast pace. Each breath cycle should last about one second. Imagine drawing in positivity and exhaling negativity. Continue for about five minutes.

Emotional Release – As you breathe, notice any surface emotions. You might feel heat, cold, tingling, or emotional releases like sadness, anger, or joy. Let these emotions flow without judgment or attachment. Use your exhale to actively release these feelings, envisioning them leaving your body with every breath.

Grounding and Integrating:

Slow Down Your Breath – Gradually slow your breathing, returning to a normal rhythm. Sit with the sensations and feelings in your body. You may feel lighter, more open, or emotionally raw. These are all normal responses.

Reflection and Journaling – When you feel ready, gently open your eyes. Take a few moments to journal about your experience. What emotions did you release? How do you feel physically and emotionally?

Closing the Practice – Finish by sitting quietly for a moment, reflecting on your intention, and noticing any changes in your inner state. Acknowledge yourself for the work you've done.

How This Enhances Your Speaking:

I designed this breathwork expedition to clear out the emotional clutter that can stifle your authenticity and expression as a speaker. By releasing trapped emotions, you:

- Enhance Authenticity: Clear emotional blockages that make you feel guarded or inauthentic.

- Improve Vocal Clarity: Release tension in the respiratory system to enhance your voice's clarity and strength.
- Increase Connection: Open up emotionally, which helps to connect more deeply with your audience.
- Boost Confidence: Reduce anxiety and increase self-assurance in your message and delivery.
- Incorporate this breathwork practice regularly, especially before important speaking engagements, to maintain clarity, authenticity, and emotional resonance with your audience.

Spark Steps

- Go to the Spark Box at www.aleyaharris.com/spark-box to get a free 30-day subscription to Mastry. Don't place expectations or judgments on your experience.
- Give the Essence Expedition a try. It is incredible the night before a presentation.
- Journal Prompts
  - Think of a time when you felt a strong emotion while speaking (nervousness, excitement, sadness). How did your breath help you manage or express this emotion? How could improving your breathwork practice enhance your ability to navigate emotions while speaking?
  - How can you incorporate breathwork into your pre-speaking routine to enhance clarity and calm? Describe a plan for a 5-10 minute breathwork session that you can do before your next speaking engagement to prepare mentally and physically.

○ Describe how mastering the flow of your breath can transform the flow of your words. How does controlling your breath change your speech's pace, tone, and clarity? How might this affect your ability to connect with your audience?

CHAPTER 9

I love this.

"Look for good things about where you are, and in your state of appreciation, you lift all self-imposed limitations—and all limitations are self-imposed—and you free yourself for the receiving of wonderful things."
—Abraham-Hicks

Transforming your perspective on challenges can change your life and your speaking. Embrace every moment with the phrase "I love this," and watch as even the most difficult situations become opportunities for growth and connection.

My whole life, I have been tall and thin. Into my early thirties, I could wear some of the same clothes I wore in high school. I had minor, socially inherited insecurities about my body, but nothing that impacted my life in a significant way. I naturally ate well, loved moving my body, and generally felt good about my appearance. Even 23 and Me said I have "elite power athlete" DNA.

And then I had a baby. While I was pregnant, I only gained 16 pounds. I was all belly and super cute. Plus, I grew a perky little bonus booty, which was a lovely push present. When Ruby Coral was born, I burned 500 calories every time I pumped, which was somewhere between four and eight times per day. I dropped the 16 pounds I gained with no effort.

Then, the pumping stopped. The sugar cravings didn't. My hormonal shifts definitely didn't. My belly started growing in a less socially acceptable way than when it was carrying my baby girl. My clothes grew uncomfortable. Chairs felt smaller. I began to choose my outfits based on whether they would hide my belly or not. When I spoke on stage, a faja or girdle was indispensable. I was more insecure than I realized. But, I didn't confront the insecurity head-on. I thought I was handling it by doing all the physical things. I started going to Hot 8 Yoga five to six times per week. I added more vegetables to my plate. I stopped buying Ben & Jerry's Cherry Garcia ice cream. I knew that in no time, I would be back to my usual self. I had never wanted to lose weight before and was in foreign territory, but I knew enough of the basics and found solace in my approach. Or so I thought.

I saw the error of my oversimplification when I was pulled out of a workshop I was facilitating because I triggered a participant. She left the room crying and embarrassed.

When I was standing in front of the room, I was wearing an oversized long denim jacket over jeans and a shirt, but I still felt exposed. For some reason, that day, I felt particularly uncomfortable in my own skin. I gave examples like, "We all know how to get the result we want. If I want to lose weight, I must stop eating three brownies after lunch." There were several similar references. The negative self-talk oozed out of me so easily, so insidiously. There are other ways to prove a point.

The participant who was triggered self-identified as being "the largest person in the room." With every negative mention of my weight, she felt like the spotlight was on her. Although I never mentioned anyone else's weight or generalized thoughts about larger people, she said my session was the straw that broke the camel's back. She had been dealing for years with societal pressures around body shape, microaggressions, and her internal relationship with herself. I brought all of that to the surface. Yes, this was excavation, but not in a positive or supportive way.

I felt horrible. If my purpose is to love people into the highest version of themselves, what the hell did I just do? I needed to start loving myself before I did even more harm to myself or anyone else.

When I went back to my hotel room after the session, I stood naked in the mirror and gave myself a good look. I put my hands on my belly and said, "I love this." I thought about all the beautiful things my stomach had done for me, including safely carrying the love of my life, Ruby Coral, into this world. I looked at the cellulite on my new booty and said, "I love this." I looked at my C-Section scar and said, "I love this." As I continued, I started to cry. I had been treating myself horribly. My body and I don't have to be enemies, and the battle that I had engaged in turned my audience members into collateral damage. I am intentionally doing better.

The incident with the workshop participant was a stark reminder of the responsibility we hold as public speakers. Our words, our examples, and the energy we emit have the power to touch every individual in the room, often in ways we might not anticipate. As speakers, our first duty is akin to the medical principle of "first, do no harm." Our responsibility extends beyond physical well-being into our audience members' emotional and psychological health. It's about ensuring that our communication uplifts, supports, and provides value, leaving the audience better than when they first walked in.

This experience deepened my understanding that effective speaking is not just about delivering content; it's about fostering an environment where every participant feels seen, heard, and respected. Our role is to facilitate growth and learning, not to exacerbate personal insecurities or societal pressures. By embracing "I love this" as a personal mantra, I learned to redirect the focus from my insecurities to my strengths, from self-criticism to self-appreciation. This shift is not just internal; it radiates outward, influencing how we connect with and impact our audience.

When we stand on stage, we are uniquely positioned to influence and inspire. By loving ourselves and embracing every part of our journey, we model the resilience and authenticity we wish to inspire in others. This approach doesn't mean shying away from our vulnerabilities; instead, it means using them as powerful tools to forge deeper connections. Our stories, including those of personal struggle and self-acceptance, can become beacons of hope and catalysts for change in the lives of those we speak to.

Being radically authentic on stage isn't about unloading every emotion or insecurity onto your audience; it's about letting the most genuine, loving version of yourself shine through. Authenticity means sharing your truths in a way that resonates and connects, not overwhelming your audience with personal grievances or negative self-talk. It's about carefully balancing transparency with the responsibility to uplift and inspire. By focusing on expressing your radically authentic, loving self, you create a space where your audience can explore their challenges and victories without feeling burdened by yours. This approach ensures that your speaking reflects your true self and fosters an environment of mutual respect, understanding, and positive transformation.

Becoming a transformative speaker involves much more than mastering the art of rhetoric or perfecting our stage presence. It's about embodying the principles of love, acceptance, and positive transformation. As we practice "I love this" in every aspect of our lives, we heal ourselves and set the stage for our audience to embark on their healing journeys. Creating a space where healing, understanding, and growth can occur, guided by our words and illuminated by our authentic presence, is the essence of being of service from the stage.

Essence Expedition: I Love This

In the journey to become more connected, purposeful, and authentically expressive, especially as speakers and entrepreneurs, shifting our perspective from complaint to gratitude and even love is crucial. Negativity takes us further away from ourselves and our audience. This Essence Expedition, inspired by the teachings of Abraham-Hicks and John-Roger, invites you to transform every challenge into an opportunity by responding with, "I love this."

Instructions:

Set Your Intention:

Begin the day by setting a clear intention. As you wake up, take a few deep breaths and affirm to yourself: "Today, I choose to see love in everything. Every challenge is an opportunity to affirm 'I love this' and find the blessing in disguise."

Recognize the Trigger Moments:

Throughout your day, stay vigilant about moments when you feel the urge to complain or express negativity. These are your triggers—common ones include receiving critical feedback, facing unexpected obstacles, or even minor annoyances like traffic or long lines.

Apply the "I Love This" Technique:

Each time you encounter a trigger, pause for a moment. Instead of reacting with frustration or disappointment, respond internally (and externally if appropriate) with "I love this." For example:

If a client sends a scathing email, before you react, say, "I love this."

If you're not hitting your sales goals, look at the numbers and think, "I love this."

If you're overwhelmed by your to-do list, take a breath and say, "I love this."

Reflect on the Shift:

After responding, notice any shift in your emotions or thoughts. How does saying "I love this" change the energy of the situation? Do you feel more empowered, lighter, or more open to finding solutions? What is the particular aspect of that situation you can find to love?

Journal Your Experiences:

Take some time to journal about your experiences using the "I love this" technique. Note the situations where it was challenging to apply and where it felt more natural. Reflect on how this approach affected your decision-making and emotional state.

Deepen the Practice with Visualization:

Close your day with a short visualization exercise. Imagine yourself handling a challenging situation with grace and positivity, saying, "I love this," and transforming the challenge into an opportunity. Feel the love and acceptance in your body, and visualize yourself making decisions for the highest good.

Using the "I love this" technique directly impacts your effectiveness as a speaker by:

Enhancing Authenticity: When you shift from complaint to love, you align more closely with your authentic self. This authenticity resonates deeply with audiences, as they can feel when a speaker is genuine and grounded.

Prevents You from Spreading Your Trauma: When you feel insecure about who you are, you can unintentionally trigger the same insecurities in your audience. Self-deprecation can be poisonous. This Essence Expedition allows you to focus on the positive aspects of yourself and the world around you so that you are inspiring instead of harmful.

Improving Resilience: By embracing challenges with love, you develop greater resilience, which is essential for handling the unexpected moments that come with public speaking and entrepreneurship.

Boosting Positive Influence: Your positive perspective will influence your audience. A speaker who can find love and opportunity in challenges inspires the audience to adopt a similar mindset, fostering a more profound and impactful connection.

Encouraging Creative Solutions: When you respond with love, you're more open to creative solutions. This mindset can lead to more innovative presentations, richer content, and engaging stories.

Reducing Stress: This technique lowers stress and anxiety, which are common issues for public speakers. A relaxed and loving state of mind helps deliver clearer, more confident, and more compelling speeches.

By integrating this simple yet profound practice into your daily routine, you prepare yourself to be a better speaker and live and lead with a heart full of love and a mind open to endless possibilities. You will capture the essence of transforming every speaking opportunity into a moment of connection, growth, and authentic expression.

Spark Steps

- Integrate "I love this" into your approach to life. Focus on the positive aspects. Allow your negative beliefs to take a back seat.
- Journal Prompts
  - What insecurities and limiting beliefs may be oozing out of you intentionally, impacting or triggering those around you? How can you find their positive aspects?
  - Reflect on when you shared a personal story or challenge in your presentation. How did you ensure this sharing was constructive and manageable for your audience? If it wasn't, what would you do differently next time to maintain this balance?
  - Recall a time when your words had an unintended negative effect on someone, similar to the workshop participant incident. What did this experience teach you about the power of your words, and how has it influenced you?

CHAPTER 10

Ideal Scene

"We cannot create what we can't imagine."
—Lucille Clifton

Vivid, intentional visions propel us toward our desired futures. Crafting and embracing these scenes can amplify your speaking career, turning aspirations into realities. From mesmerizing an audience on stage to effortlessly booking gigs and creating a Radical Spark Signature Talk™, use your imagination and emotions to manifest success. Shape your speaking journey with clarity, confidence, and the power of intention.

I remember it like it was yesterday. I was standing on a stage, presenting to a corporate audience of about 150 people at a large tech company based in Santa Barbara, CA, and the room was dead silent. Each audience member was hanging on my every word, leaning in to absorb every nuance of my story. You could hear a pin drop. I saw eyes moisten and jaws relax as the human beings in the audience found themselves in the image I was creating through my presentation experience. It was a profound moment of deep connection and the beginning of a healing journey for many. I was standing in my purpose, which was to help them stand in theirs.

As the words flowed from my mouth, I thought, "OMG! I did it! This is exactly the scene I envisioned!" It took all my willpower to stay present and maintain the momentum of my delivery. I wanted to pause and marvel at the power of my words and intentions, but I knew I had to keep going and finish strong.

About a year before this moment, I had created an Ideal Scene that went something like this: "I am standing on stage, delivering a presentation to a captivated audience. The event organizer has compensated me more generously than ever before, and I feel a rush of excitement stepping into the next level of my career. I am confident, powerful, connected, and clear. I am a master of my craft." Until that moment on stage, I had almost forgotten about the Ideal Scene I had crafted, but there it was, unfolding into reality right before my eyes.

That experience hooked me on the power of intentionality in shaping my career as a professional speaker. I began to sit quietly and get clear about what I wanted, methodically drawing these desires into my reality. Manifestations came in their own time, but each brought the same exhilarating sense of empowerment that I felt on stage that day.

As a speaker, your role extends beyond delivering content; you are in the business of transformation. This transformation is about what you facilitate for your audience and what you create in your own life. Aligning with your Radically Authentic Self allows you to take inspired action and create shifts in your personal and professional experiences. The more you achieve your goals and build momentum, the more your confidence grows—in yourself, your abilities, and your craft.

Your success on the stage starts way before you ever step foot into the spotlight. Mostly, it is about where your mindset is, where your energy is, and how you've been working and conspiring with the Universe to help bring you what you want. In this book, I am leading you through a tangible and tactical experience of becoming a professional speaker and the energetic options you have to help amplify your efforts in this physical body. One of my favorite tools for doing that is the Ideal Scene.

Your Ideal Scene is something that you write in the present tense that helps ground your visualization. You write it as something that is happening to you now and most importantly, you feel the feelings of what is happening to you in that Ideal Scene. You intentionally choose to feel good.

The things that are attracted to you are a match to you. So, if you are feeling nervous, anxious, angry, not good enough, and sad, the things and the people that you will attract into your life will help prove you right and validate the feelings that you are currently having. You can intentionally feel something different and, by extension, have a different experience.

Using your Ideal Scene, you can intentionally give yourself the feeling you have when you are successful, when you are the best public speaker in the world, and when you are captivating an audience. You can give yourself that feeling and begin attracting things, experiences, and additional feelings that match. By doing that, your Ideal Scene becomes your manifested reality.

Your Ideal Scene is a way of working with the Universe and the tools at your disposal to make your speaking dreams a reality. Your Ideal Scene is a picture of what life looks like after you become a fully booked professional speaker. Write your Ideal Scene in the present tense, and keep it to three to five sentences because we will do something called programming after you've created it. Your Ideal Scene could be about how you feel on the stage. It could be about your overall speaking career. It could be whatever you need to flow forward and move through the limiting belief that is holding you back so that you can be successful.

Here is the exact Ideal Scene that I wrote for myself that has helped bring me great success:

"Every day, I wake up to another email from an event organizer requesting to book me to speak to an audience of my ideal clients. I joyfully travel worldwide as a respected professional speaker, delivering my messages on stages where I feel adored and appreciated. I am paid at least $10,000 for each speaking engagement and have more than enough money to leave a legacy of abundance. This or greater for the highest good. Thank you."

That last line, "This or greater for the highest good. Thank you." is something that I encourage you to include in your Ideal Scene because, spoiler alert, you don't know everything. There could be something even better for you related to your vision. The most important thing to remember as you create and use your Ideal Scene is that you feel the joy, excitement, and accomplishment of the scene you are describing, consciously raising your feelings to match this Ideal Scene.

Here's how you can harness the power of your words to shape your speaking career:

1. Craft Your Ideal Scene: Just as I did, sit in a quiet space and envision your perfect speaking scenario. Write it down in vivid detail, focusing on how you want to feel and the impact you want to have.

2. Feel the Future Now: Don't wait for the future to feel successful or confident. Start embodying those emotions today. This alignment dramatically increases your chances of attracting the opportunities you desire.

3. Reflect and Adjust: Regularly revisit your Ideal Scene. Is it still what you want? As you grow and evolve, so too might your

vision. Adjust as necessary, always keeping your feelings and intuition as your guide.

4. Share Generously, Without Overwhelming: Remember, your journey can inspire others. Share your experiences and the lessons you've learned without overwhelming your audience with too much personal detail. Let your authenticity shine through in a relatable and uplifting way.

By using your words and intentions to shape your experience, you uplift yourself and those who come to hear you speak. Each speech is an opportunity to transform—a chance to turn your Ideal Scenes into your reality, one word at a time.

Essence Expedition: Ideal Scene

It is easier to manifest something when you have a clear picture of what it looks like. Because you are a powerful creator, you can detail exactly what you want and expect it to come to pass. By developing your Ideal Scene and then feeling it in the present tense, you are calling in the cooperative components of the Universe to make your vision a reality.

An Ideal Scene is a short paragraph written in the present tense about a vivid and specific point of time you would like to bring into your current physical experience. It is an alignment and manifestation tool that helps clear the communication channel between you and the Universe.

You can develop an Ideal Scene about yourself on stage, booking a gig, or even the experience of crafting your Radical Spark Signature Talk™. It is important to feel connected to what you create and stay focused on the solutions it brings to your life, not the current challenges you are trying to solve. As Abraham-Hicks often says, "Problems and solutions have very different vibrations." The goal of the Ideal Scene is to get you to attract vibrationally the things that will bring you joy and relief.

As you craft your Ideal Scene, there are a few ground rules to make it effective:

- Write about your own experience. Don't try to control other people. For example, you could say, "I am standing on stage, feeling powerful and confident." I would avoid saying something like, "The audience loves me." Leave their emotions to them. This is about you.

- Write in the present tense and in the first person. That would sound like "I feel at peace" instead of "I felt at peace."

- Include how you feel and feel the feelings. Think of the feelings as the activators of your Ideal Scene. Examples of good-feeling words are "relaxed, peaceful, happy, elated, and worthy."

- Avoid including conditional phrases and timing. Here is an example of what not to do: "It is June 2026, and I feel amazing after I just booked my first 5-figure speaking engagement. Because of the booking, I can now take my dream vacation." A better way of saying that would be, "I just booked my first 5-figure speaking engagement and feel amazing. I am about to go on my dream vacation." The second option eliminates the time specificity and causality. Attempting to control your manifestation too tightly may add unnecessary friction to your manifestation process.

- Keep it short. If you decide to program your Ideal Scene, which I highly recommend, you will say it 100 times without stopping. You don't want this experience to overwhelm you because you've written multiple paragraphs. Keep your Ideal Scene to 3-5 sentences and make each word count.

- End your Ideal Scene with this: "This or greater for the highest good. Thank you." You want to keep yourself open and available for amazing things that you haven't thought of. By ending with gratitude, you raise your vibration to match your Highest Self.

The process of creating your Ideal Scene:

1. Sit in a quiet place and think of something to make you feel successful as a professional speaker.

2. Imagine the moment of your highest emotional connection with the success point. Where are you? How are you feeling? What are you smelling? Keep thinking about it until it feels clear.

3. Double down on the feelings. Begin to name them silently to yourself. Repeat the names of the feelings and magnify their intensity. You may start to sense your face begin to smile or other parts of your body having pleasant reactions. Those are signs you are on the right track.

4. When you feel like the scene you've created in your mind is palpable, transfer it onto the page. As you write, don't worry about length just yet. Your goal is to write until you feel that you have captured what you just saw inside of you.

5. Review what you wrote and edit it until it is 3-5 sentences. When you feel like you've completed your Ideal Scene, read

it aloud and make sure that it captures the feelings you had when it first came to you. Adjust as needed.

6. Optional but highly recommended: Program your Ideal Scene to increase its effectiveness. Read your Ideal Scene aloud 100 consecutive times without stopping. I suggest you download a counter app on your phone to keep track. It also works well if you can do it while you are moving. You could safely pace the room or rock back and forth. Try to feel the feelings as you speak.

7. When you are complete, display your Ideal Scene somewhere where you will see it daily. Read it at least once daily and continue to feel the positive feelings in the present.

A Note about Programming Your Ideal Scene

Programming is kind of an interesting experience. You're going to read your Ideal Scene without stopping 100 times. That's why I said to keep it short.

The first maybe one through 30 times of reading your Ideal Scene, you'll be like, "Oh my God, why am I doing this? I don't want to do this." Then you'll probably get a feeling similar to a runner's high where you are getting into it. You start feeling the good feelings. You might end up saying it faster or find that you begin to relish the words as they come out of your mouth. Ride that high as long as possible.

Usually, around the 75th time of saying your Ideal Scene, the doubts will start coming in. You may find your mind saying things like, "I don't need to finish it. I don't *really* need to do this. Oh, this is hard. I'm thirsty. I'm tired. This doesn't work." You might even start to feel dizzy or a little nauseous. I encourage you to breathe through any negative feelings and let them go. The shift you feel is simply your Ideal Scene anchoring into your Spirit. Make sure it takes root by fully reaching 100 repetitions. When I program Ideal Scenes, I sometimes do 102, just in case I miscounted.

Once your Ideal Scene is programmed and set, I advise you to drink water and wash your hands and face to clear out residual energy. After you program your Ideal Scene, read it to yourself every morning or multiple times throughout the day. Feel the good feelings. See the visuals that match in your mind's eye. The more concrete your Ideal Scene is to you, the more likely you will be able to manifest your professional speaking career.

Of course there will be work in the physical that you have to do, but when you only operate in the physical as a speaker, you are not as good of a speaker. The work you do should be from inspired action, not fear or sheer willpower. That's why, in the very beginning, I told you to channel. That's why I've been taking you through these Essence Expeditions. I want you to use all your tools at your disposal, physical and spiritual, to become a sought-after, successful, wealthy, accomplished, and respected professional speaker.

Here are a few examples of Ideal Scenes:

Captivating Presence on Stage

I am standing on the stage, feeling powerful, confident, and deeply connected to my authentic self. The bright lights warm my skin, and the energy of the room fills me with excitement. I sense the engagement of every person in the audience as I deliver my speech with clarity and passion. My words flow effortlessly, and I feel a harmonious blend of excitement and calm. I am fully present, enjoying the interaction, and I feel elated as I see the impact of my words reflected in the eyes of my listeners. My heart is open, and I am in perfect alignment with my message, radiating inspiration and confidence. This or greater for the highest good. Thank you.

Effortless Gig Booking

I am sitting at my desk, feeling a wave of accomplishment and joy wash over me. I've just confirmed a new speaking engagement with a prestigious organization, and I feel valued and excited about the opportunity. My email inbox shows a signed contract and a note of thanks from the event organizer, praising my professionalism and the alignment of my topics with their audience's needs. I feel a deep sense of gratitude and anticipation for the collaboration, knowing that this is exactly the type of work I love to do. The process was smooth and affirming, reinforcing my belief in my path and the value I bring as a speaker. This or greater for the highest good. Thank you.

Crafting My Radical Spark Signature Talk™

I am in my creative space, surrounded by notes and inspirations, feeling a surge of creativity and clarity as I develop my Radical Spark Signature Talk™. The words seem to write themselves, each slide and story falling into place perfectly. I feel proud and excited as I see my unique experiences and insights weave into a powerful, deeply personal, and universally resonant presentation. I can hear the audience's reactions—laughs, gasps, and applause. This talk truly reflects who I am and what I stand for, and I feel an immense sense of purpose and joy as I bring it to life. I am grateful for this process, which feels more like a celebration of my journey than work. This or greater for the highest good. Thank you.

An Ideal Scene is more than just an exercise in positive thinking; it is a tool for transformation. As you engage with your Ideal Scene, remember that your role as a speaker extends beyond sharing information; it's about leaving your audience enriched and uplifted. By embodying the principles of love, acceptance, and positive transformation in your preparation and delivery, you ensure that your presence is a gift to your listeners. Through an Ideal Scene, you're not just rehearsing your future; you're actively creating a space where every word you speak builds bridges and transforms lives.

Spark Steps

- Create your Ideal Scene
- Program your Ideal Scene
- Keep track of your manifestations and stay in gratitude
- Journal Prompts
  - Think about a recent challenge or obstacle you faced in your speaking career. How could you rewrite that experience as an Ideal Scene, transforming the challenge into an opportunity for growth and success?
  - Reflect on the process of turning your Ideal Scene into reality. What steps are you taking to manifest these visions? How does this process make you feel, and what lessons are you learning?
  - How does your Ideal Scene help you align more closely with your Radically Authentic Self? Describe how this alignment influences your presence and impact as a speaker.

CHAPTER 11

Reading to Speak

"Think before you speak. Read before you think."
—Fran Lebowitz

Turning the pages can turn up your impact as a speaker. Your next great idea could be waiting to be inspired by someone else's words.

Standing in rooms with some of Google's brightest minds during my tenure as a Google Vendor Partner, I felt the gnaw of imposter syndrome. Despite being surrounded by people who were just like me—educated, accomplished, and highly skilled—the aura of Google's prestige made me doubt my own capabilities.

I remember the feeling of working at Google distinctly: a blend of admiration and intimidation as I walked the halls with what I assumed were the planet's most intelligent people. Each step felt like a testament to my presumed inadequacy. Yes, I am fully aware of how toxic my mentality was. I wish I had internalized Theodore Roosevelt's famous quote, "Comparison is the thief of joy," but I still had a long way to go in my confidence journey. It was more than slightly uncomfortable to always be "one of" the smartest people in the room rather than the smartest person. This discomfort was palpable among my peers as well, though none of us spoke of it—at least not at first.

It wasn't until the Director of the Google Food Program, my de facto boss, emailed us a mandatory reading list, designed to push our thinking and enhance our perspectives, that I started to see a shift in myself and my colleagues. This wasn't just any set of books; it was an eclectic reading list, carefully selected to challenge us, bring us together, and give us a common ground from which to grow not only as professionals but also as people.

The transformation began subtly, but the books proved to be a lifeline thrown into the turbulent sea of our doubts. As we delved into these texts, our discussions moved from mere information exchanges to vibrant, insightful dialogues that celebrated diverse viewpoints and unique interpretations.

One of the first books we read together made me realize that I wasn't alone in feeling like an imposter. The shared experience of reading the same material didn't just level the intellectual playing field—it created a space for vulnerability. We started to share our thoughts on the books and our feelings about the work we were doing, the pressures we felt, and the silent battles we were each fighting.

These conversations were turning points. I recall a particularly striking session where a colleague admitted feeling like an imposter. That confession, made during one of our book discussions, opened the floodgates. Suddenly, everyone was sharing, nodding in agreement, offering their stories and support. We realized that we were all dealing with similar feelings, regardless of our backgrounds or achievements. The books gave us the language and the courage to express our vulnerabilities and to find strength in our shared experiences.

This newfound camaraderie and understanding had a profound effect on my confidence. I began to see that knowledge wasn't just power—it was empowerment. Armed with insights from our readings, I became more adept at handling challenges, more articulate in meetings, and more confident in my role. Reading had transformed from a solitary activity into a communal bridge that connected us in our shared human experience.

About a year after I started with the reading list, I was given the opportunity to speak at the Google Vendor Partner Meeting in May 2015. It was one of the first times I spoke in front of a large crowd. Not only were Googlers there, but the room was full of my parent company's competitors. Before the journey of the reading list, I would have been terrified, but I remember stepping out in front of that room, feeling comfortable in my skin, and realizing that I belonged there.

After my presentation, I received high praise from my parent company's CEO. He said, *"Aleya Williams [my maiden name] presented this afternoon at the Google Partner meeting in Mountain View to about 90 Compass people (a slight exaggeration), the entire Google Food Team, a handful of other competitors, and about a half-dozen Guckenheimer team members. She was FANTASTIC! Funny, informative, got her message across with great clarity, and literally rocked the place. I could not have been more proud. She is a STAR. I was most impressed. She discussed a variety of brand-related topics and had a very good exercise on how to respond to client feedback in a very structured and purposeful way.*

"I thought the entire senior leadership team at Guckenheimer should know how well she represented us today. And, I decided to copy our fine clients (Michiel, Linda) who gave her the chance to shine. Thank you for giving Aleya the opportunity today. I think we all won."

My Google bosses/clients responded with, *"You all should be very proud! Aleya rocked the house."* and *"Totally concur that Aleya is indeed an incredible superstar. She is it! Love, love, love having her on our joint team."*

It's safe to say that reading helped my speaking.

Over the years since that moment, as I grew more comfortable in my skin and more secure in my knowledge, my approach to speaking changed as well. I realized that as a speaker, my responsibility extends beyond delivering content; it involves connecting with my audience on a fundamental level. Each speaking engagement became an opportunity to practice what I had learned—to weave the insights from my readings into relatable, engaging, and transformative stories.

This journey of reading and discussion wasn't just about combating imposter syndrome; it was about enriching my approach to communication and leadership. It taught me that reading can be a powerful tool for personal and professional development, especially for public speakers who must connect with and inspire their audiences. Now, I approach each speaking opportunity not just as a chance to impart knowledge but as a moment to share wisdom, inspire change, and foster a sense of community and understanding.

Reading is a foundational tool for speakers, enriching their discourse and deepening their impact. For a speaker, each book, article, or TEDx talk acts as a mirror and a window—a mirror reflecting one's inner thoughts and a window into the experiences of others. When you read, you are not just absorbing information but engaging with ideas that can serve as a springboard for your insights. Each piece of literature provides a point of reaction, a basis from which your unique perspectives can leap forward and resonate with authenticity.

Literature offers a spectrum of lenses through which speakers can explore and understand not only their true selves but also the diverse authentic selves of others. It deepens the empathetic connection a speaker can forge with an audience, grounding abstract concepts in relatable human experiences. By engaging with various texts, speakers gain a richer vocabulary and a broader pool of knowledge to draw from, ensuring that they always have something substantive and engaging to say.

Understanding the historical context of your topics through a thorough literature review allows you to honor what has come before while contributing new thoughts and insights. This review is not merely academic due diligence—it is an act of respecting the intellectual landscape and finding your unique voice within it. It helps you identify gaps in the conversation, spaces where your unique perspective and authentic self fit perfectly, enabling you to add fresh layers to the dialogue.

For example, I learned the Ani-Hu chant from reading the works of John-Roger. Through his teachings, I understood the power of spiritual exercises and how they could propel entrepreneurs past their limitations and toward their potential. I incorporated Ani-Hu in my work and was blown away by how well my audiences accepted it. I have received many follow-up communications that detail how individuals who have heard me speak and applied Ani-Hu have seen vast improvements in their business life. Reading and understanding your place in the world enhances your credibility and ensures your contributions are both relevant and revolutionary, pushing the boundaries of understanding and inspiring your audience to explore new ideas.

I invite you to explore the transformative power of reading and how it can enhance your speaking abilities. By engaging deeply with diverse materials and reflecting on their lessons, you can elevate your intellect and your capacity to connect and communicate. Whether you're addressing a room of corporate professionals or a community workshop, let your readings inform your speeches and turn every presentation into an experience that resonates and inspires.

Essence Expedition: Reading to Speak

As a speaker, your words are your tools, and the breadth of your knowledge defines the depth of your toolbox. I designed this Essence Expedition to expand your intellectual horizons and enhance your speaking prowess. It's not just about reading books; it involves immersing yourself in a diverse range of materials—TED Talks, podcasts, articles, and more—that challenge your thinking and refine your communication skills. This practice will provide you with a wealth of content to share and deepen your understanding of various perspectives, enriching your ability to connect with and inspire your audience.

The goal is to get some "outsight" to help shape your "insight."

Outsight is the practice of seeking perspectives outside of your personal experiences to enrich your understanding and expand your worldview. Outsight informs your understanding and enhances your ability to relate to and address a wider audience. It acts as a bridge, connecting internal insights with external realities, facilitating a deeper connection with your audience by backing up your personal experiences and anecdotes with broader, globally relevant content.

By integrating outsight into your learning regimen, you ensure that your speaking is grounded in personal truth and resonant with universal appeal, making your messages more impactful and relatable.

Here's how I recommend getting some outsight:

1. Set Your Learning Goals.
   Begin by defining what you want to achieve with your reading and learning. Are you looking to deepen your expertise in a specific field, or are you seeking to broaden your knowledge base? Setting clear goals will help you select materials that align with your objectives.

2. Create a Diverse Reading List
   Compile a list that includes books, articles, podcasts, and TED Talks across various subjects. Include classics in your field,

contemporary thought leaders, and content that pushes your boundaries. Utilize the reading list provided by my director as a starting point, accessible via the link at the end of this chapter.

3. Schedule Regular Learning Sessions
   Dedicate specific times in your weekly schedule for reading and listening. Whether it's an hour each morning, a podcast during your commute, or a TED Talk on your lunch break, make this a non-negotiable part of your routine. I like listening to YouTube and TED Talks while driving to hot yoga. Do whatever makes sense for you.

4. Engage Actively
   As you read or listen, take notes, highlight key points, and jot down any ideas or questions that arise. This active engagement helps deepen your understanding and retention of the material. If you are driving or on the move, record voice notes or call and leave yourself a voice message.

5. Reflect and Relate
   After each session, spend a few minutes reflecting on how what you've learned can be applied to your speaking. How does this new knowledge enhance your understanding of your topics? How does the knowledge help articulate points of contrast you've experienced in your life? How can it be used to enrich your presentations or discussions?

6. Share and Discuss
   Whenever possible, discuss what you've learned with peers or mentors. When I was at Google, I found this particularly valuable. Sharing insights and debating concepts is a powerful way to cement your knowledge and refine your opinions.

7. Incorporate into Your Speaking
   Begin weaving the insights and information you've gathered into your speeches and presentations. This will not only keep your content fresh and relevant but also demonstrate your commitment to growth and learning.

By committing to reading to speak, you are expanding your intellectual repertoire and enhancing your effectiveness as a communicator. This Essence Expedition will equip you with a richer language and a more comprehensive range of anecdotes, examples, and evidence to draw upon, making your speeches more engaging and impactful. As you continue to explore new ideas and perspectives, remember that each piece of knowledge adds a layer to your foundation as a speaker, helping you to inspire and connect with your audience on deeper levels.

Remember, you can often find the support tools for transformational speaking in the pages of a book or the words of a talk. Embrace this journey of continuous learning, and let the knowledge you gain illuminate your path to becoming a speaker who informs, truly enlightens, and inspires.

I was able to dig up the reading list that my director gave me many moons ago, and I included my favorite books in the Spark Box at www.aleyaharris.com/spark-box. I've also added some of my new picks that have helped me over the years. Feel free to use this list as a jumping-off point. Happy reading!

Spark Steps

Set your content consumption plan. Will you read for 30 minutes while you eat lunch? Will you listen to a TED Talk while you clean up after dinner? Pick a time of day or a task you already complete to pair your content consumption with and stick with it.

- Choose your first content piece to consume. Don't overthink it. The goal is to get started and make it a regular habit.
- Get together with a crew of folks and create an outsight club. Talk about what you are learning and how it impacts your life and craft.
- Journal Prompts:
  - How can you blend outsight with your personal stories to enhance your speeches? Write about a specific topic you speak about and list external sources that could provide additional depth or a new angle to your narrative.
  - How has feedback from others influenced the types of materials you seek out? Describe a time when audience reaction prompted you to explore a new topic or deepen your knowledge in a particular area.
  - What are your learning goals for the next six months, and how do these goals align with your speaking objectives? Outline a plan for selecting reading materials and other resources that support these goals.
- Check out the Spark Box at www.aleyaharris.com/spark-box for a list of my favorite books.

CHAPTER 12

Go Outside & Play

"Play!"

—**Ruby Coral Harris**

Rediscover the joy of play and its powerful impact on your creativity and authenticity as a speaker. By embracing playfulness, you open yourself to Spirit, get into the flow, and bring a fresh, engaging energy to your presentations.

Energetic. Perfectionist. Gregarious. Smart with a touch of know-it-all. Spiritual. Tall. Sexy… all words that accurately describe me.

Playful. Lighthearted. Laissez-faire… all words you would not find anywhere in my astrological chart, not even tucked away in one of my houses. If you hear someone say, "Oh, I know Aleya! She is so chill," slowly back away. We clearly have never met, and you might be in a catfish situation.

I have always wanted to play more, to be less serious. However, when I try to get a hobby, I find a way to monetize it or turn it into something serious. I liked to cook, so I went to Le Cordon Bleu and became a professional chef who traveled around the world with celebrity clients. I liked to write blogs, so I became a copywriter and eventually a Strategic Storytelling Consultant who built a company around the words that flow from my energy field to the page. I recently started hot yoga, and one of the teachers suggested that I become a teacher. I think you can see how this is going to play out.

As an adult, I have struggled with the concept of play. Being so serious has caused my stress levels to become so bad that I experience hives, full-body itching, and restless leg syndrome every night before bed. Luckily, my toddler is an expert at playing. She can see the simplest thing and giggle with pure joy. She runs and commits her antics for no reason other than wanting to have a blast. She climbs on everything, even things she's not supposed to, just because it feels good. She has become my official Professor of Play, and class is in session daily.

The more I look at the world through her lens, the more I stop giving every breath and action a job to do, I begin to feel my connection with Spirit deepen. Spirit is not serious. It doesn't participate in stress, struggle, trauma, or drama. Spirit is perpetually unbothered and full of fun. Life is supposed to be fun. When you are having fun, you are in tune with Spirit and can more easily hear its guidance.

Opening yourself to Spirit isn't always about chanting, sitting in silence, or meditating in the traditional sense; it's also about embracing joy and the lightheartedness of play. In the flow of play, you align effortlessly with Spirit, your source of inspiration and creativity. It is essential for any speaker seeking to connect genuinely and dynamically with their audience.

Engaging in play as an adult might sound unconventional, especially if you've molded yourself into a figure of perennial seriousness, but it's a powerful form of meditation. When you play, you enter a state of flow—losing track of time and self-consciousness. This flow state is akin to a meditative state where you are fully present in the moment, not hindered by past worries or future anxieties. This mindfulness amplifies your connection to Spirit, allowing you to channel your most authentic self during your presentations. Because of these moments, your speaking can transcend mere performance to become a shared experience of joy and discovery with your audience.

Essence Expedition: Go Outside & Play

I encourage you to play. Not "Oh, I need to get my steps in, so I'll go for a walk." Head to the beach for some volleyball with friends or swing from the monkey bars at the park. Play is an activity without a greater aim. Enjoy actively engaging in life for the fun of it.

Here are some suggestions to get you started with having adult playtime (not *that* kind. Sheesh! Get your mind out of the gutter… although that could be fun, too):

1. Revisit Childhood Joys. Think back to what made you happiest as a child. Was it painting, dancing, playing a sport, or building with blocks? Reintroducing these activities into your life isn't about regressing but reconnecting with a part of yourself that reveled in creativity and joy without pressure. My jam has always been singing, so I downloaded a Karaoke app on my phone and belt out Mariah Carey until my heart's content.

2. Try New Hobbies That Have No ROI. Choose activities that don't create pressure to perform or succeed. Activities like pottery, knitting, or gardening can be therapeutic and fun without the temptation to monetize the skill. I recommend NOT scrolling through Etsy and getting any ideas of monetization.

3. Engage in Improvisational Activities. Improv classes are a fantastic way to nurture your spontaneous side and enhance

your speaking skills through playful expression. The rules of improv emphasize positive acceptance—saying "yes, and"—which fosters a supportive environment for creativity.

4. Play with Kids. Just as Ruby Coral is my Professor of Play, playing with children can be one of the best ways to learn how to let go and enjoy the moment. Their innate ability to find joy in the simplest activities can be incredibly infectious and inspiring. Got a friend that needs some babysitting? It is time to volunteer.

5. Join a Recreational Sports Team. Adult sports leagues are great for fun and fitness. They also encourage teamwork and communication, critical skills for any speaker. I have never been a sports person, but this may be perfect for you.

6. Set a "Play Time." Just as you might schedule work tasks, deliberately schedule time for play. It could be anything from a 15-minute break to play a game on your phone to a full day at the beach or hiking.

Through play, you enrich your spiritual and emotional well-being and enhance your effectiveness as a speaker. Play helps dissolve the barriers of overthinking and self-critique many speakers face, allowing you to deliver your talks with more natural enthusiasm and authenticity. Embrace play, and watch how it transforms not just your speaking style but your entire outlook on life and work, making each more joyful and impactful.

Spark Steps

- Choose a play activity that makes you feel good.
- Set a Play Time for yourself at least a few times per week.
- Journal Prompts
  - Think about the last time you lost track of time because you were having fun. What were you doing? How can you incorporate more of this activity into your regular schedule?
  - What are the barriers that prevent you from engaging in playful activities? Is it time, guilt, perception, or something else? How can you overcome these barriers to make room for more joy and spontaneity in your life?
  - In moments of play, have you ever felt a deeper connection to something greater than yourself? Describe that experience and explore how it might influence your perspective on speaking and connecting with audiences.

CHAPTER 13

Embrace Your Authentic Self on Stage

"Authenticity is the daily practice of letting go of who we think we're supposed to be and embracing who we are."
—Brené Brown, *The Gifts of Imperfection*

Step into the spotlight with confidence by embracing your authentic self. Own your true identity, share it boldly from the stage, and create deeper connections with your audience while amplifying your impact.

As we wrap up Section 1: Get Real, it's crucial to understand that genuinely compelling speakers aren't just well-versed in their subject matter—they have something valuable to add to the conversation. They are open channels, conduits for authentic messages that resonate deeply with their audience. Being an effective speaker is more than just delivering a polished talk; it's about staying connected to your core and allowing that connection to shine through in every word you say.

Great speakers prioritize connection above all else. They are vigilant about keeping their core unburied and open, recognizing that this openness allows them to connect with their audience genuinely. To do this, you will need to embrace vulnerability as a powerful tool. By sharing your authentic self, including your struggles and triumphs, you invite your audience to do the same. This mutual vulnerability fosters a deep sense of trust and engagement.

Throughout this section, you've embarked on a journey to excavate your authentic self and channel the highest version of you. You've learned to shed outdated narratives and replenish your spirit, enabling you to connect deeply and resonate with your audience. Remember, vulnerability is not a weakness; it is your greatest strength. It unlocks your potential as a speaker, allowing you to touch hearts and inspire minds.

As we move forward to the next section, remember these principles. Stay open, stay connected, and continue to embrace your vulnerability to build the foundation of your Radical Spark Signature Talk™. By doing so, you will not only deliver powerful presentations but also transform lives—starting with your own.

Spark Steps

- Use the Essence Expeditions to build new routines. By using the tools you resonate most with consistently, you will begin to experience a profound expansion of your abilities as a speaker.
- Plan a personal retreat where you remove distractions and put several Essence Expeditions into practice. Think of these few hours as an investment in your future career as a sought-after professional speaker.
- Check out the Spark Box at www.aleyaharris.com/spark-box for tools to support you in these Essence Expeditions and beyond.

Section 2
Get Clear

"Clarity of writing indicates clarity of thinking"
—Timothy Ferriss

Uncover the power of your personal stories to craft a Radical Spark Signature Talk™ that captivates and inspires. In this section, you'll delve into the art of storytelling, using your unique experiences to connect with your audience profoundly. Through detailed guidance and practical exercises, you'll learn to transform your authentic journey into compelling narratives that highlight your struggles, triumphs, and key insights. Get ready to streamline your story and create a presentation that informs and transforms.

The number one question I get from Spark the Stage™ students is, "Do I have a story to tell?" My answer is always a resounding yes! Every single one of us has a unique journey filled with experiences, challenges, and triumphs that can inspire and motivate others. No matter how ordinary you might think your story is, it holds the power to connect, resonate, and transform. Telling a story that helps others is always a story worth telling.

In this section, we'll explore how to uncover and shape those stories into compelling narratives that captivate your audience. We'll delve into the nuances of your experiences and show you how to extract the valuable lessons and insights that can make a real impact. Remember, your authenticity and willingness to share your journey make your story powerful.

By now, you've begun to explore and embrace your authentic self, unearthing the core of who you are and what you bring to the table as a speaker. This foundational work is crucial, but now it's time to take the next step—getting crystal clear on your story and how to share it effectively.

In this section, we'll explore the process of developing your Crisis Stories. These stories are the heart of your Radical Spark

Signature Talk™, designed to resonate deeply with your audience and establish you as a relatable, credible, and compelling speaker. We'll explore how to craft narratives that capture attention and inspire and motivate your audience to take action.

Building on the self-discovery and authenticity work from Section 1, we will now focus on translating those insights into powerful stories that highlight your journey, struggles, and triumphs. Our journey from this point forward isn't about storytelling for entertainment; it's about creating meaningful connections with your audience through shared experiences and lessons learned.

As we move through this section, you'll learn how to effectively utilize the Crisis Story Framework™, develop Success Celebrations, gather your unique gifts, and identify your Golden Thread—the overarching theme that ties your entire presentation together. I designed each step to help you build a cohesive, impactful narrative that aligns with your core message and engages your audience from start to finish.

By the end of this section, you'll have a solid foundation for your Radical Spark Signature Talk™, ready to be fleshed out into a structured, engaging presentation. So, let's get started and dive into the transformative power of your stories.

CHAPTER 14

Crisis Story Development

"The wound is the place the light enters you."
—Rumi

I designed each Essence Expedition in this book to guide you through self-exploration and personal growth, which are crucial steps in preparing you to craft and share your own Crisis Stories effectively. If you've been doing the work up until now, you should be ready to delve deep into your past experiences, emotions, and lessons learned, allowing you to uncover and articulate the core elements that will form the foundation of your Crisis Stories.

The Essence Expeditions help equip you with a clear understanding of how your experiences have shaped you and how you can use them to inspire and guide others. By connecting deeply with your journey, you ensure that when you stand to speak, your story resonates not just as a recount of events but as a beacon of empathy, inspiration, and understanding that can profoundly impact your audience.

The Essence Expeditions and journal prompts also serve as a rehearsal space to experiment with different ways of expressing your story, helping you find the most impactful method to connect with your audience. This preparation is key to ensuring that when you share your story, it is well-received and fosters a genuine connection.

I told you there was a method to my madness. Now, you are ready to move forward with Crisis Stories, Success Celebrations, Gift Gathering, and identifying your Golden Thread.

Before diving into the specifics, it's essential to understand how these elements relate to your broader speaking framework. Integrating these components isn't just about choosing interesting anecdotes; it's about strategic alignment with your core message and mission as a speaker and business owner.

Here's how to make these elements work for you in a larger framework:

Framework Alignment

First, ensure that each story or element you choose underpins the larger framework or theme of your presentation or the methodology you use with your clients. Your framework serves as the skeleton of your talk, while your stories are the flesh that adds life and relatability. Each story should exemplify a key point in your framework, making abstract concepts concrete and emotionally engaging. You want your stories to support the grander idea of what you want to be known for in the world.

Choosing Your Stories

When selecting which stories to share, consider their relevance and impact. A good story for your framework isn't just emotionally compelling; it should directly illustrate the lessons or values that are pivotal to your message.

For Crisis Stories, choose those that reflect profound transformations relevant to your audience's needs and your speaking goals. For Success Celebrations, pick moments that epitomize peak achievements aligned with your framework's aspirations. Gift Gathering involves identifying personal strengths and insights gained through experiences, which should bolster the credibility of your message and enhance your authority as a speaker.

The Golden Thread

The Golden Thread is the underlying theme that connects your stories and the primary purpose of your talk. Identifying this thread helps ensure coherence and a strong narrative flow in your presentation. It allows the audience to navigate your stories and grasp the overarching message without getting lost in isolated anecdotes.

By consciously aligning your stories with your speaking framework, you ensure that each narrative element is a standalone tale and a strategic tool that enhances your overall message. This alignment clarifies your presentation for your audience and strengthens your effectiveness as a speaker, ensuring that each story moves your audience closer to the transformation you promise.

Now, let's dive into the nitty gritty.

Crisis Story Overview

A Crisis Story is a meticulously crafted autobiographical narrative that leverages personal challenges and triumphs to inspire, motivate, and equip audiences on their transformational journeys. Its purpose is to share lessons from lived experiences and connect deeply with listeners by demonstrating resilience and the possibility of change.

Crisis Stories are the foundation of a Radical Spark Signature Talk™. They provide the emotional connection, authority of lived experience, and proof of your ability to empathize with your audience. They humanize you while also elevating you to the level of an expert because you have overcome the challenges in the story, lived to tell the tale, and are there to help the audience do the same.

Various Crisis Stories could be used multiple times throughout a Radical Spark Signature Talk™, as the overall theme of an entire presentation, or to inform the "why" behind your work. I have given keynotes that were only one Crisis Story using my Crisis Story Framework™. After giving one of those keynotes to a small audience of about 75 women, I had seven come up to me afterward in tears, telling me how much they resonated with the story, felt inspired, and were encouraged to step more fully into their power. Crisis Stories and the Crisis Story Framework™ are highly effective tools for making deep connections with your audience.

However, the audience is not the only one who benefits. By going through the Crisis Story Framework™, you may begin to have epiphanies and develop a greater understanding of yourself, your purpose, and the general themes of your life. You could look at the list of your Crisis Stories and realize that all these stories have been keeping you in a similar pattern, and you want to talk about how you are breaking that pattern. You could notice that you find a similar resolution through each crisis or learn a different facet of the same lesson. You may discover what your Radically Authentic Self is trying to whisper keys to your greater calling to you through each trial and tribulation.

The Crisis Story development process is vital, and I wouldn't ask you to dive into your past and remember a bunch of negative stuff if it wasn't. I encourage you to give your Crisis Stories lots of thought and to remember that you are amazingly resilient. I congratulate you on enduring each of your crises and still being here to tell the story. That's huge. You have risen from adversity. You have triumphed. You have overcome.

Sharing your Crisis Story will feel interesting, but I want you to remember that the most helpful lessons come from your lived experience. The entire purpose of getting into this professional speaking thing is to be of service. However, I do want to say a disclaimer before we get into the Crisis Story Framework™: You don't want to tell something that you are still living as a trauma. You want to tell something you have healed from, that you feel comfortable saying from the stage, and that will not re-trigger you.

I don't want you to hurt yourself emotionally. Also, I hate it when speakers cry on stage because of their own material. It feels manipulative because an audience is coming to see a speaker who has prepared, rehearsed, and adeptly presents the content. They are expecting a professional. If the speaker is crying because of their own stories, it either means they are not ready to tell that story yet, or they're using tears to evoke an emotional response from the audience that is more about the speaker's need to be validated than helping the audience heal and grow.

With that said, we're going to get into unearthing your Crisis Stories. But I want you to remember that you've gone through a lot. If you are not ready to tell that deepest, darkest secret, don't. There are other things that you can tell and draw lessons from to serve your audience.

But don't take this as an excuse to stay too surface level or avoid speaking about the life conditions that have shaped you into who you are. Remember, secrets don't help anyone. They weigh you down, and the lack of information and inspiration could rob an audience member of the exact thing they needed to take the next step in their journey. If you are being called to tell the secret, you will feel that it is eager to come into the light.

If you keep your story to yourself, no one else can benefit. When you convert your secrets and crises into stories and share them from the stage, they become beacons of empathy, inspiration, and understanding. They transform from personal sagas to communal triumphs.

I am going to walk you through my Crisis Story Framework™ in three steps so that you can build inspiring, motivating, and clarifying narratives.

1. Crisis Collection

2. Lesson Excavation

3. Story Crafting

First, you take stock of all you have overcome, especially the particularly messy bits. Then, you dive into each crisis to extract the lessons and morals. Finally, you mold these experiences into a powerful narrative.

Let's break down each step.

Crisis Collection

Make a list of all of your crises, both big and small. Some of my crises include moving through postpartum depression, experiencing temporary physical disability due to stress and burnout, a failed membership that I spent $30,000 on that grossed $0, and being laid off twice. You could have similar crises, or yours could look wildly different. Some crises from previous Spark the Stage™ students include falling off their bikes as kids, divorce, traumatic brain injury, and loss of loved ones.

All of these are crisis stories, and they are all valid. Your goal is to list about five to ten of your own. All you have to do is write a quick bullet point note for each one. We will develop them later. You're not trying to build the story yet. You're just trying to remember the incident.

Lesson Excavation

A crisis is only valuable because it taught you something. If you simply talk about what you've been through without articulating the lessons you've learned, you are trauma dumping, not inspiring. The stage is not the appropriate place for your therapy session. The lessons and the moral are why you are telling the story. Although the story happened on your journey, you are using it to guide someone else on theirs.

Examining your list of crises, are there three or four that have a common theme? Perhaps it is a shared lesson, or they illuminate your purpose. They could also be related to your work. Once you identify the three or four from the list that call to you, ask yourself these critical questions about each one:

- What did I learn from this experience?
- How did enduring this crisis change my perspective or approach to life?
- What strengths did I discover in myself through this crisis?

Next, take those same three to four stories and define your three-step path to victory. What did you do to go from mad to happy? From sad to peaceful? Break down your first stage, the bulk of the work you did in the middle, and then how you made a final push toward success. These three steps could eventually turn into three main points in a section of your Radical Spark Signature

Talk™, or they could be the overarching sections of your Radical Spark Signature Talk™ in its entirety. It depends on how you use your Crisis Story.

Story Crafting

Now that we know what the crises are, what we learned, and how we navigate our path to success, it's time to articulate the "so what" for our audience. When someone is listening to your story, they will be asking themselves, "What's in it for me?" Tailor your narrative in a way that resonates with their experiences and expectations. Your story should be about your journey and offer insights, lessons, or inspiration that your audience can apply in their own lives.

Every audience member is a narcissist with a short attention span (that includes you and me when we are in the audience, too). That means they need your presentation to be about them now, five minutes from now, and five minutes from then to remain engaged in what you are saying. They already have thousands of excuses not to pay attention. From the allure of their electronic devices to their daydreams to chit-chatting with their neighbor, it is nearly effortless for them to tune you out. However, when you tell a story they can immediately see themselves in, your audience is much more likely to pay attention.

Your audience may not have experienced what you have. Find universal themes in your personal stories that echo in the lives of your listeners. Whether it's overcoming adversity, facing fears, or achieving personal growth, many can relate to these experiences.

Emotion is the lifeblood of a good story. A story that evokes emotions—joy, sadness, hope, or inspiration—stays with the listener long after your speech ends.

To craft a compelling Crisis Story, use these four steps:

1. Set the scene with time and place. For example, "It was a hot summer day in 2003, but my hands were cold as ice..."

2. Articulate the crisis and the problem that caused it. Make sure to describe how it made you feel and why it was just plain wrong that you had to deal with that issue.

3. Insert the three steps on how you resolved the problem, the outcome, and/or moral. This step is where you can be the most service to your audience. Let them know how you did it so they can, too. Share what you learned so they can benefit from your experience.

4. Relate the Crisis Story to the broader presentation context. When you are telling a crisis story from the stage, you need to use it to articulate the overall purpose of the presentation or illustrate key points to anchor them in the hearts and minds of your audience.

I could sit and tell you data, stats, and numbers all day long, and you won't remember them. But you will remember, feel, and connect with me, the content, and the presentation because of the stories that I tell. Having multiple connected stories throughout the presentation is how you create a compelling presentation.

The opening story of this book and many of the stories from Section 1 followed the Crisis Story Framework™. You were being frameworked, and you didn't even know it! Now that you are part of the in-crowd let me break down a story for you.

Step 1: Set the scene – time and place.

"I died in a cold operating room on November 7, 2022."

Step 2: Articulate the crisis and the problem that caused it.

"I had just simultaneously given birth to my beautiful baby girl, Ruby Coral, and watched the woman I had become up to that point fall into darkness. Over the next ten months, that darkness consumed me, and I slipped into the bowels of postpartum depression.

"I felt ashamed of my feelings, as if I was failing at the very first step of motherhood. A practical crisis compounded this internal conflict: as a business owner, my mental state directly impacted my work. My revenue dwindled, adding financial stress to my already heavy burden."

Step 3: Insert the three steps on how you resolved the problem, the outcome, and/or moral.

"I was able to see my way through the darkness by doing three things:

1. Asked for and accepted help.

2. Shared my story.

3. Clarified and obsessed over my vision for the future."

Step 4: Relate the Crisis Story to the broader presentation context.

"Today, I will talk to you about how Asking, Sharing, and Clarifying can help you become a more resilient entrepreneur, no matter what you face."

In this example, I am using the Crisis Story to set the foundation for the rest of the presentation. Each of the three steps in step 3 of the Crisis Story Framework™ is a section in the presentation. The first section of the presentation would be about asking, the second about sharing, and the third about clarifying. In each individual section, I could elaborate on using another Crisis Story that dives into the details of the original story, specifically relevant to that step.

One thing I want to underscore is that the story is about my journey through postpartum depression, but the topic of the presentation is related to being a resilient entrepreneur. The specifics of your stories do not need to relate to your content. It is about using the overarching lessons of your stories to help articulate common experiences, mindsets, or behaviors. Don't count out your stories because they are not within the same context as your Radical Spark Signature Talk™ content.

Now, it is your turn to create your first Crisis Stories. You can use these stories in your Radical Spark Signature Talk™, or you may not. The goal is first to get comfortable using the framework. Once you do, you will be able to tell Crisis Stories with very little preparation.

When you openly share your crises and challenges, you pave the way for presentations that are informative and transformative. As you step onto your next stage, whether it's a boardroom, a seminar, or a virtual meeting, remember the power of your story. Embrace the vulnerability and courage it takes to share your crises. Your experiences, resilience, and journey are not just yours alone—they are a gift to your audience, a means to inspire, connect, and empower.

Let's not keep our stories as secrets tucked away. Instead, let's share them with the world, using our narratives to create presentations that are impactful and a catalyst for change. Remember, your story can move hearts and minds—don't underestimate the power of your crisis transformed into a story of triumph.

Spark Steps

- Collect your crises, extract the lessons, and craft your stories.
- Develop at least three crisis stories to use in your Radical Spark Signature Talks™.
- Try to use the Crisis Story Framework™ a few times in daily conversation to get used to letting your thoughts flow in that structure.
- Check out the Spark Box at www.aleyaharris.com/spark-box for a downloadable guide to the Crisis Story Framework™.

CHAPTER 15

Success Celebration

**"Success leaves clues. Go figure out what someone
who was successful did, and model it."**
—Tony Robbins

Your Crisis Stories are incomplete until they help you illustrate how you've overcome a situation. The success you experience in your own life is your greatest credibility marker. You have done it. You are the authority. You have conquered the experience. Knowing that also boosts your confidence.

Although I encouraged you to include your morals and lessons learned in your Crisis Stories, sometimes it is difficult to feel your wins when your starting point is a deficit. Success celebration helps you shift perspectives to build better stories. Examining your life's journey from this perspective can often help you more clearly understand the outcomes of your crisis. Success Stories also help you remember that the Universe is always conspiring for your good.

Take some time to list your successes.

Pat yourself on the back for the fantastic things you've done and experienced. Yes, some of your successes may have resulted from the crises you just outlined, but some could have been amazing surprises or wonderful experiences.

Right about now, you may be thinking, "I've already gathered my life's stories. I am going to skip this chapter. Aleya will never know." You're right. I really won't. But you may feel a bit battered, raw, or down after Crisis Story Development. Vulnerability can be exhausting, and dredging up your past crises can be demotivating. Listing your successes can boost your confidence and help reset your focus back into the positive.

In fact, listing successes is one of my favorite things. I even keep a running list with me. I whip it out any time I feel like an imposter or insecure. Think how handy a written success list could be the first time you step out onto a big stage and begin to spiral with questions like, "Who am I? Why am I here? Am I good enough?" You could quickly peek at the list and change your inner monologue. You might say things instead, like, "Don't get it twisted. I have accomplished this. I've done that. I am unstoppable." That is a much better place to be.

When it comes to speaking, rarely do I see people struggle with putting together the actual presentation, outline, or slides. The struggle I see most often is a confidence issue. They ask themselves, "Why would people listen to me? What story do I have to tell? Does my story matter?"

You have untapped greatness inside of you, and the keys could be in the success you didn't acknowledge and in the things you overlooked because they were just part of your normal mode of operations. By writing those things down, recognizing them, and owning them, you will find that you are much more successful than you've given yourself credit for. You are worthy of a listening ear. You may say, "Oh, everybody gets awards," or "Everybody triumphs over adversity," or "Everybody opens a business." No, they do not.

Don't minimize yourself; celebrate yourself. You deserve to feel confident based on what you've accomplished. Past accomplishments are a big part of the antidote to imposter syndrome and feeling self-conscious on stage. Use success to step into your power so you can step onto that stage and light it up.

So go ahead and gather your successes. Connect them as needed to your Crisis Stories and feel good. Keep your success list handy because, my friend, you are stepping onto a new journey and might just need it.

Spark Steps

- Collect your success stories and make your success list.
- Adjust your Crisis Stories as needed so that the full weight of your success is obvious.

CHAPTER 16

Gift Gathering

**"The purpose of life is to discover your gift;
the work of life is to develop it; and the meaning
of life is to give your gift away."
—David Viscott**

Although it may not always feel like it when you're going through crises, you also gain gifts. As you go through each experience, you gain the gifts of resilience, patience, intelligence, and knowledge. I want you to gather the gifts you have received from your Crisis Stories and your successes.

I also want you to gather your innate gifts, those you were born with. These are the ones that others recognized, even when you were little. You may not have received compliments for them. Maybe your teachers said you were annoying or troublesome because of some of your inherent behaviors. Remember how I always got in trouble for using my voice? I used to view it as a problem, and now it is one of my most considerable gifts. I use my voice on my podcast, the *Flourishing Entrepreneur Podcast*, on stage, in Spark the Stage™, with my strategic storytelling clients, and in one-on-one coaching. My voice is my biggest money-maker. It is a gift. Over time, I have refined my natural gift into something exemplary.

Oh, I am sorry. I just called myself exemplary. Did I just say that I'm good at something? I should have downplayed my gift, right? I should have cowered in false humility because that makes other people feel comfortable. That is so wrong, but it is how many of us treat our gifts. We hide them so we can people please. Does that sound like you? I hope this experience of gift gathering will help you unabashedly own your gifts.

I want you to say things like, "Yes, I am a good cook," "I am good at numbers," or "When I step into a room, people take notice." If you can't own it when it's just you by yourself, you won't be able to step into it on stage or use your gifts for your benefit. In our society, especially with women, we're taught that if we state our gifts, we're being egotistical. Articulating your gifts is not about ego; it is about confidence. I want you to step into the power of the gifts you earned, the gifts you've experienced, and the gifts you were born with.

Gift gathering, very similar to the success celebration process, is a confidence-boosting tool, but it does some other beautiful things. It helps you refine your why, especially when you look at the gifts you were born with. It enables you to put together the puzzle pieces. You may look at your life and realize that you've gone through things that all seem related to helping others overcome their fear of failure. You may have failed several times and are no longer afraid of failure. What a gift that is.

I've always been drawn to the stage. When I was younger, I was a dancer, played the violin and piano, and relished acting and singing in school plays. Once I dove into my gifts, I began to realize that part of my why is to help other people find their voice and share their stories. It comes so naturally to me, and it is a valuable skill.

If you have difficulty pinpointing your gift, think about the things that make it hard for you to relate to others. For example, I have a tough time coaching people to overcome stage fright because of my natural gift of loving the spotlight. I have to use other stories and experiences where I do feel self-conscious to empathize. There were certain times when I felt a lack of confidence on stage, but those times have always been when I felt unprepared. If something is preventing you from relating to others in a specific area, that is a clue to your gifting.

When you can understand your gifts, your stories are not just about overcoming and triumph; they become about your hero's journey of transformation, using and finding the tools that you need at the moment to become successful.

Spark Steps

- Make a list of your gifts.
- Adjust your Crisis Stories as needed to incorporate your natural and earned gifts.

CHAPTER 17

The Path to Developing Your Radical Spark Signature Talk™

It's time to carve out a you-sized space in the world by encapsulating the core of who you are and how you serve others through thought leadership in a Radical Spark Signature Talk™.

Your stories are critical elements to developing your Radical Spark Signature Talk™, but you just have random stories that may not seem to connect right now. That's OK because we will tie your stories, methodologies, and how you make money together to create a powerful Radical Spark Signature Talk™ presentation that will position you as a helpful, relatable expert.

A Radical Spark Signature Talk™ is an impactful and profoundly personal presentation that conveys your unique message, expertise, or story to an audience. As you develop your thought leadership, your Radical Spark Signature Talk™ is what you become known for. It encapsulates your core message and defines your personal or professional brand. Your Radical Spark Signature Talk™ is the foundation of the narrative you want to lead and the jumping-off point for your products, services, business lines, and future talks. This type of talk resonates deeply with the audience, creating an emotional connection and driving home a clear, impactful takeaway. It leverages your personal experiences, insights, and passions to inform, inspire, and motivate the audience.

You have already started down the path of developing your Radical Spark Signature Talk™ by creating your Crisis Stories and amplifying them with your successes and gifts.

Congratulations on taking the first steps to creating a powerful presentation. Here's what the rest of the journey looks like:

1. Stories: Develop your Crisis Stories and amplify their effectiveness with your successes and gifts (check!)

2. Golden Thread: Search for themes within your stories that resonate with the message you want to be known for and support how you want to make money.

3. Controlling Idea: Your Radical Spark Signature Talk™ should convince the audience to adopt a new idea, participate in a paradigm shift, or change their behavior. Your Controlling Idea defines the purpose of your Radical Spark Signature Talk™ and outlines your perspective.

4. Story Framework: Articulate the journey you will lead your audience on during your Radical Spark Signature Talk™ and ensure it has critical elements to motivate toward action.

5. Outline: Create a clear structure for your presentation. Don't worry, I've got a great one that audiences love, and I will walk you through it.

6. Slides: Build simple slides to illustrate your key points and supplement your stage performance.

As you develop your Radical Spark Signature Talk™, remember that the content should be at the intersection of your audience's problem and your passion because no one cares about your passion until that passion helps them solve their problem. I don't want you running off creating great content that doesn't lead to you getting paid.

We've talked all about you up until now—your crises, your successes, and your gifts. Now, we need to intersect all of your goodness at the point where your audience has a real problem, a problem that you can solve because of who you are, what you have been through, and your knowledge. The goal is to get them to pay you to solve that problem by paying you to speak or buying your products or services.

CHAPTER 18

The Golden Thread

Tie all of your Radical Spark Signature Talk™ elements with an ideological through line. If your ideas are disjointed or your Radical Spark Signature Talk™ tries to prove too many thoughts simultaneously, you will not be as effective as a speaker.

Imagine your Radical Spark Signature Talk™ as a beautiful nighttime scene, where each key point or story is a lantern hanging delicately from a single, continuous string. This string is your Golden Thread, and it plays a crucial role in providing cohesion and structure to your talk. Just as pulling the string would cause each lantern to collapse together into a unified line, so too should pulling on the Golden Thread of your presentation bring all elements of your talk into one coherent message.

This metaphor underscores the importance of the Golden Thread in ensuring that every piece of your talk, every story, and every central point not only stands on its own for its beauty and illumination but also aligns perfectly with the others, creating a harmonious and impactful whole. By threading your narrative this way, you ensure that your audience can follow the path you've laid out without getting lost, each point lighting the way to the next, leaving them with a clear understanding and memorable impression of your core message.

The Golden Thread is the unifying theme that ties together various stories, insights, and messages into a coherent narrative. It makes your presentation not just a collection of disjointed parts but a compelling journey with a clear, purposeful direction. The Golden Thread is the backbone of your talk, guiding the audience through your narrative and ensuring that every element contributes to the overarching theme.

The Golden Thread is essential for maintaining coherence throughout your presentation. The consistent theme or message runs through every aspect of your talk, helping your audience understand how each part contributes to the whole. This continuity is crucial for keeping the audience engaged and making your presentation memorable and impactful.

For example, in a talk on the power of resilience, the Golden Thread might be the idea that overcoming obstacles is not about avoiding failure but learning and growing from challenges. Every story and piece of evidence you present should tie back to this central theme, reinforcing and illuminating your core message at every turn.

To identify your Golden Thread, start by reflecting on the primary purpose of your talk. Ask yourself: What is the central theme that connects all parts of my presentation, the thing that unifies my most impactful stories? This theme should be broad enough to encompass all your main points yet specific enough to give your presentation a clear focus.

Think about a classic film like *The Matrix*. The Golden Thread in this narrative could be the theme of reality versus illusion. Each character's development and every plot twist and conflict explores this theme, making the film a cohesive exploration of what it means to confront and challenge one's perceived reality.

In your presentations, the Golden Thread serves a similar purpose. It's your promise to your audience that you will reward their attention with a clear, cohesive understanding of your topic.

Keep revisiting your Golden Thread as you develop your presentation. With each new piece of content—a story, statistic, or slide—ask yourself how it enhances or illuminates the Golden Thread. This constant attention ensures that your presentation is cohesive and that every element serves a purpose within your narrative.

By understanding and effectively using the Golden Thread, you ensure that your presentation tells a coherent and compelling story. This strategic narrative thread transforms your presentation from a mere collection of ideas into a powerful, unified message that resonates deeply with your audience.

The Golden Thread is a crucial element in developing your Radical Spark Signature Talk™ for several compelling reasons:

1. Provides Coherence and Unity: The Golden Thread is the central theme that ties all elements of your talk together. It ensures that each part of your presentation, from anecdotes and data to visual aids and calls to action, is unified under a coherent theme. This unity helps prevent your talk from becoming disjointed or confusing, ensuring your audience can easily follow along and understand the overall message.

2. Enhances Audience Engagement: Maintaining a consistent theme throughout your talk helps the audience stay engaged. The Golden Thread acts as a narrative guide, leading them through your presentation and helping them see the relevance of each point as it contributes to the bigger picture. This continuous thread keeps the audience interested and invested

in your message, as they can see how each component is part of a larger story.

3. Increases Memorability: A Radical Spark Signature Talk™ should be memorable, and having a clear, strong Golden Thread helps achieve this. When your talk revolves around a central theme, it becomes easier for the audience to remember your message. The Golden Thread provides a simple, repeatable idea that they can recall and share with others, enhancing the impact and reach of your talk.

4. Facilitates Emotional Connection: The Golden Thread often embodies the emotional core of your presentation. It's not just what you talk about but the underlying emotion or passion that drives your message. This emotional resonance is crucial for connecting with your audience on a deeper level, making them feel inspired, motivated, or moved by your talk.

5. Guides Content Selection: When developing a Radical Spark Signature Talk™, one of the challenges is deciding what to include and what to leave out. The Golden Thread helps you make these decisions by acting as a criterion for relevance and impact. If a potential content piece doesn't align with or enhance the Golden Thread, it likely doesn't belong in your talk. Your Golden Thread helps keep your content focused and powerful.

6. Supports Persuasion and Influence: The ultimate goal of many Radical Spark Signature Talks™ is to persuade or influence the audience. A well-defined Golden Thread helps build a strong argument or persuasive case throughout the presentation. Each element of the talk contributes to building this case, making it more compelling and convincing by the conclusion.

7. Encourages Personal Reflection and Development: For speakers, identifying and articulating a Golden Thread requires deep reflection on their values, beliefs, and the key messages they want to share. This process can be a powerful personal development tool, helping speakers clarify their thoughts and refine their perspectives.

By weaving a Golden Thread throughout your Radical Spark Signature Talk™, you ensure that the presentation is impactful, engaging, and a true representation of your core message and personal brand. The Golden Thread is an indispensable tool for any speaker aiming to create influential and memorable speeches.

I realize that the Golden Thread concept may be a challenge to grasp, so I've included a few more examples to help as you think about developing the Golden Thread for your Radical Spark Signature Talk™.

Famous Books and Movies

1. *To Kill a Mockingbird* by Harper Lee
   ○ Golden Thread: The enduring impact of empathy and moral integrity in confronting social injustices. This theme is woven through Atticus Finch's defense of a wrongly accused man and his efforts to teach his children about kindness and justice, regardless of the prevailing prejudices of their time.

2. *The Matrix*
   ○ Golden Thread: The quest for truth in a world filled with deception. This theme is central to the protagonist's journey, as Neo discovers the reality behind the seemingly normal world and chooses to fight against the controlling

powers, illustrating the broader message about awakening and questioning reality.

3. *Inception*
    ○ Golden Thread: The thin line between reality and illusion, and the deep impact our subconscious has on our perceptions and experiences. This theme recurs as characters navigate layers of dreams to achieve their missions, raising questions about what is real and how our dreams influence our waking life.

Talks by Entrepreneurs

I realize that it can be challenging sometimes to relate your work to that of a film or book, so here are some Golden Threads that an entrepreneur could possibly use for their Radical Spark Signature Talk™.

1. Talk on Innovation by a Tech Entrepreneur
    ○ Golden Thread: True innovation requires creating new products and thinking differently about solving problems. The entrepreneur can weave this theme through personal stories of breakthroughs and setbacks, highlighting how unconventional thinking was crucial to their success.

2. Talk on Resilience by a Startup Founder
    ○ Golden Thread: Resilience isn't about avoiding failure but embracing it as a stepping stone to success. The entrepreneur could demonstrate this through their journey of overcoming repeated failures and how each setback provided valuable lessons that led to eventual success.

3. Talk on Sustainable Business Practices by an Eco-Friendly Business Owner
    ○ Golden Thread: Sustainability isn't a limitation but an opportunity for innovation and leadership in business. The entrepreneur could illustrate this theme by sharing how adopting eco-friendly practices not only helps the planet but also improves business operations and opens up new markets.

Each of these examples of Golden Threads helps to ensure that the narrative stays focused and impactful, driving home the central message in a way that resonates with the audience and leaves a lasting impression.

Spark Steps

- Develop the Golden Thread for your Radical Spark Signature Talk™. If you are unsure, develop a few and then read them aloud. Go with the one that makes you feel the most excited.
- Check out the Spark Box at www.aleyaharris.com/spark-box for a short guided meditation on determining what "yes" and "no" feel like in your body to help boost your confidence as you decide on your Golden Thread.

CHAPTER 19

Controlling Idea

"Invisible threads are the strongest ties."
—Friedrich Nietzsche

Once you have your Golden Thread, you can build it out further into a Controlling Idea. The two concepts are related but not the same. Let me break it down.

A Golden Thread refers to the overarching theme or message that connects and weaves through the entire narrative of your talk. It's the central, unifying thread that ties all elements of your presentation together and ensures coherence and consistency. The Golden Thread helps the audience follow along and understand how each part contributes to the whole. It's like the spine of your story, providing structure and direction.

A Controlling Idea, while related to the Golden Thread, focuses more on the specific message or lesson you want your audience to take away from your presentation. Your Controlling Idea includes your point of view and is what you are trying to convince your audience of. It's the concise expression of your talk's main argument or point. If you were writing a school paper, it would be your thesis statement. The Controlling Idea is the guiding principle for what you include in your presentation—it dictates the relevant details and how your audience should interpret them. Essentially, it's what you want your audience to believe or do as a result of hearing your talk.

In practical terms, the Golden Thread keeps your narrative aligned and cohesive from start to finish, ensuring every element of your talk contributes to this overarching theme. The Controlling Idea, on the other hand, is more about the impact and takeaway, ensuring that the content not only aligns with the Golden Thread but also supports the specific action or belief you are advocating.

When developing your Radical Spark Signature Talk™ or any presentation, clarifying both elements is crucial. Your Golden Thread ensures that your narrative flows logically and engages the audience. At the same time, your Controlling Idea focuses on the outcome, ensuring that the talk is impactful and leads to the desired audience transformation or action.

To structure your Controlling Idea, use the formula: **Purpose x Subject x Your Point of View.**

- Purpose clarifies what you want your audience to take away
- Subject specifies the topic of discussion
- Your Point of View presents your unique stance or insight

This format sharpens your message and makes it actionable and directly connected to your objectives as a speaker.

Using that format, let's define the Controlling Ideas for the earlier examples:

1. *To Kill a Mockingbird* by Harper Lee
    - Purpose: Inspire action against social injustice
    - Subject: Empathy and moral integrity
    - Point of View: Empathy and moral courage are essential to overcoming societal prejudices.
    - Controlling Idea: "Inspire action against social injustice through empathy and moral integrity because they are essential to overcoming societal prejudices."

2. *The Matrix*
   - Purpose: Encourage questioning of perceived realities
   - Subject: Reality vs. illusion
   - Point of View: Questioning our reality is crucial to escaping manipulation and achieving freedom.
   - Controlling Idea: "Encourage questioning of perceived realities in the context of reality vs. illusion because it is crucial to escaping manipulation and achieving freedom."

3. *Inception*
   - Purpose: Promote self-awareness
   - Subject: Impact of the subconscious on reality
   - Point of View: Understanding our subconscious is crucial for truly grasping how our realities are shaped.
   - Controlling Idea: "Promote self-awareness regarding the impact of the subconscious on reality because understanding it is crucial for truly grasping how our realities are shaped."

4. Tech Entrepreneur on Innovation
   - Purpose: Foster innovative thinking
   - Subject: The role of mindset in innovation
   - Point of View: Innovation stems more from how we think than what we do.
   - Controlling Idea: "Foster innovative thinking by focusing on the role of mindset because innovation stems more from how we think than what we do."

5. Startup Founder on Resilience
   - Purpose: Encourage embracing failures
   - Subject: The value of resilience in business

- ○ Point of View: Embracing failures is foundational to long-term success.
- ○ Controlling Idea: "Encourage embracing failures within the context of business resilience because seeing them as foundational to success changes how we approach challenges."

6. Eco-friendly Business Owner on Sustainable Practices
   - ○ Purpose: Advocate for sustainable business practices
   - ○ Subject: Sustainability as a driver for business innovation
   - ○ Point of View: Sustainability challenges us to innovate and lead in the market.
   - ○ Controlling Idea: "Advocate for sustainable business practices highlighting how sustainability challenges us to innovate and lead in the market."

The Controlling Idea plays a crucial role in the development of your Radical Spark Signature Talk™ for several key reasons:

1. Focus and Clarity: The Controlling Idea serves as the central thesis of your talk. It provides a clear, concise statement of what you are arguing or advocating. This clarity helps you stay focused while preparing your presentation and ensures that every element of the talk contributes directly to this main idea. This focus is essential for maintaining the audience's attention and making your message clear and understandable.

2. Guidance for Content Selection: With a well-defined Controlling Idea, you can more easily decide what to include in your talk and what to leave out. This guiding principle ensures that all included stories, statistics, and arguments are relevant and contribute meaningfully to the main message.

It acts as a filter, helping you avoid digressions or irrelevant details that can dilute the impact of your presentation.

3. Enhances Audience Engagement: A strong Controlling Idea captures and holds the audience's attention by clearly stating what they will learn or understand by the end of your talk. It sets the stage for a compelling narrative journey, where the audience is eager to see how you will support, illustrate, and conclude the idea you've presented.

4. Strengthens Persuasion: The Controlling Idea is your main argument in persuasive talks. You reinforce your argument and enhance your persuasive impact by articulating this idea clearly and returning to it throughout the presentation. Each piece of evidence or anecdote is seen in the light of this central argument, making your overall case more potent and more convincing.

5. Facilitates Emotional Connection: A powerful Controlling Idea often resonates emotionally with the audience. Depending on its nature, it can inspire, challenge, or provoke thought. This emotional engagement is crucial for memorable and impactful speaking, transforming the presentation from a mere transfer of information to an influential experience.

6. Aids in Structuring the Presentation: The Controlling Idea helps structure the overall presentation. It provides a logical framework that guides the arrangement of your content. Starting with an introduction of the idea, moving through supporting arguments or narratives, and culminating in a strong conclusion that reinforces the Controlling Idea, the structure of your talk becomes more coherent and impactful.

7. Promotes Consistency: The Controlling Idea ensures consistency in tone, style, and message throughout your talk. This consistency helps build trust and credibility with your audience, as they receive a unified message from start to finish.

In essence, the Controlling Idea is not just a part of your Radical Spark Signature Talk™; it is the backbone that supports everything from the initial concept to the final delivery. It ensures that your talk is informative, engaging, persuasive, and memorable.

Once your Controlling Idea is defined, integrate it clearly at the beginning of your presentation. Reinforce it throughout by aligning all stories, data, and discussions to support this idea. Conclude by summarizing how everything presented substantiates the Controlling Idea, urging your audience toward the action or belief you are advocating. Don't worry; we are about to walk you through an outline that will help you do just that.

By utilizing this structured approach to your Controlling Idea, you ensure your presentation delivers information and persuades and resonates deeply with your audience, guiding them toward a clear and impactful conclusion.

Spark Steps

- Develop the Controlling Idea for your Radical Spark Signature Talk™.

CHAPTER 20

The Spark Storytelling Framework™: Igniting Connection Through Story

> "Stories constitute the single most powerful weapon in a leader's arsenal."
> —Dr. Howard Gardner

The Spark Storytelling Framework™ is a structured approach to crafting compelling narratives. It will help you create emotionally resonant and intellectually stimulating presentations that captivate and inspire their audiences.

We now have all of the key elements of your Radical Spark Signature Talk™. We just need to pull everything together. First, we will use a storytelling framework to guide the narrative, and then translate that framework into an outline.

You might have just told yourself, "I'll just skip to the outline. I am ready to get this thing done already!" But that would be a mistake. Skipping straight to the outline without first crafting your story can lead to a Radical Spark Signature Talk™ that lacks depth and emotional connection. The storytelling part allows you to explore and clarify the core message, ensuring that every element of your talk resonates with the audience and supports the overall narrative. This foundational step is crucial for creating a compelling and cohesive presentation that informs, inspires, and motivates your audience. Without this, you risk delivering content that may be well structured but ultimately forgettable and less impactful.

Hopefully, I've convinced you that the story part is necessary.

The framework we will use is called The Spark Storytelling Framework™. I designed this framework to help speakers and entrepreneurs ignite a deep connection with their audiences by crafting stories that resonate, inspire, and motivate. In line with the goals of being a radically authentic professional speaker, this framework is built around the concept of lighting a spark within the audience, transforming passive listeners into engaged participants in the speaker's journey.

The Spark Storytelling Framework™

1. Kindle the Desire

Build an emotional and intellectual desire for change or action. Highlight the motivations that compel the hero (potentially the audience member) to embark on their journey.

Questions to Consider:
- What is it that your audience wants?
- What are the internal and external reasons compelling the journey?

- How can you articulate any initial reluctance and the means to overcome it?
- What emotional hooks can you use to deepen the audience's investment in your presentation?

2. Illuminate the Challenge

Hook the audience by presenting a relatable problem that sets the narrative in motion. Introduce the setting and the initial challenge you or your intended hero face.

Questions to Consider:

- What specific problem or challenge will capture the audience's attention?
- What emotional state has the problem activated within them?
- How does this problem relate to what the audience desires or aspires to achieve?
- What are the stakes involved if this problem remains unresolved?

3. Fuel the Journey

Discuss the journey, including trials, tests, and conflicts along the way, and the lessons learned that can empower the audience.

Questions to Consider:

- What key obstacles or conflicts have you or will your hero encounter?
- Which specific Crisis Stories from your experience illustrate these challenges and lessons effectively?
- How do these stories help progress the narrative toward a resolution?

4. Ignite the Transformation

Identify the core message or breakthrough insight that will change the audience's understanding or perspective. It should link to your Controlling Idea and Golden Thread.

Questions to Consider:

- What are the critical turning points in your narrative?
- How do these turning points lead the audience from their current state to where they need to be?
- How does this transformation align with the overall promise of your Radical Spark Signature Talk™?

5. Radiate the Resolution

Outline how the transformations achieved can be applied practically by the audience.

Questions to Consider:

- What are the key outcomes or resolutions you want the audience to experience?
- How can these outcomes be practically applied in the audience's life or work?
- What long-term impacts do you envision these lessons having on the audience?

6. Share the Spark

Motivate the audience to implement what they've learned in their own lives and use it to improve the lives of others. Focus on ongoing engagement and using your presentation as a jumping-off point for their ongoing journey.

Questions to Consider:

- What specific actions do you want the audience to take following your talk?
- What is a grander sense of altruism you can inspire in your audience based on your content?
- How can you ensure the audience remains engaged with the content or with you as a speaker?

The Spark Storytelling Framework™ is not just a tool for structuring content; it's a comprehensive approach that ensures your message resonates deeply and elicits the desired emotional and intellectual response from your audience.

The Spark Storytelling Framework™ ensures consistency and cohesion in your Radical Spark Signature Talk™. Before diving into the specifics of your talk, the Spark Storytelling Framework™ helps establish a strong foundation by aligning your core message across all elements of your presentation. By defining the stages, from Illuminating the Challenge to Sharing the Spark, you create a narrative flow that prevents the common pitfall of disjointed content, where sections of the talk feel unrelated or contradictory. The framework reinforces your Golden Thread so your audience isn't confused or disengaged.

The Spark Storytelling Framework™ starts by setting the stage with a challenge that engages the audience immediately by tapping into their emotions—desires, fears, frustrations, or aspirations. This emotional hook is critical for maintaining audience interest and making the message stick. By carefully planning how to kindle and fuel the journey through emotional highs and lows, you ensure the audience remains invested throughout the talk.

Using the Spark Storytelling Framework™ encourages you to consider the audience's perspective and needs constantly. I designed each framework stage to reflect on how the audience will receive and process the information. This audience-centric approach ensures that the talk delivers value, addresses the audience's pain points, and speaks directly to their experiences, making your message more impactful and relatable.

By structuring your presentation to ignite transformation and radiate resolution, you effectively lead the audience through a carefully curated argument or story that builds towards a logical and powerful conclusion. This methodical build-up enhances your persuasive power, as each segment of the talk reinforces your Controlling Idea and drives home the reason for change or action.

The culmination of the Spark Storytelling Framework™ with the Share the Spark stage inspires action. By preparing your talk with this framework, you ensure that by the end of your presentation, you have informed, inspired, and equipped your audience to take confident steps toward achieving their goals. The focus on actionable outcomes is crucial for talks that drive personal, professional, or societal change.

The Reflect the Lessons and Share the Spark stages are about distilling and consolidating the insights gained throughout the talk into memorable takeaways. These sections ensure the audience leaves with information and valuable lessons that are easy to recall and share, extending the influence and impact of your talk beyond the immediate presentation.

By integrating the Spark Storytelling Framework™ before outlining your talk, you ensure that the structure, content, and delivery are strategically aligned to create a powerful, persuasive, and memorable presentation. This preparation sets the stage for a successful talk and reinforces your role as a thoughtful, insightful, and impactful speaker.

Example of the Spark Storytelling Framework™ in Use

I know it is difficult to understand the concept without seeing it in action. To that end, I'd like to introduce you to my fictitious friend named "Jane" and show you how she might use the Spark Storytelling™ Framework.

Jane Smith is an experienced executive coach who has spent over two decades guiding leaders through some of the toughest challenges in their careers. Her extensive background in crisis management, combined with her empathetic and strategic approach, has helped numerous executives navigate turbulent times with resilience and grace. Jane's talk, "Leading Through Crisis: Transformative Leadership in Turbulent Times," is designed to provide actionable insights and inspiration for leaders at the helm during challenging situations. Her framework will be built around three pivotal crisis stories from her coaching experience, each illustrating different aspects of effective leadership in times of crisis.

Let's look at how Jane used the Spark Storytelling™ Framework to outline the narrative of her talk.

1. Kindle the Desire

- **Desire:** Leaders want to guide their teams through crises effectively, emerging stronger and more resilient.
- **Context:** "In today's volatile business environment, crises are inevitable. As leaders, our greatest desire is to navigate these turbulent times successfully, keeping our teams motivated and our businesses thriving."

2. Illuminate the Challenge

- **Challenge:** The main challenge is maintaining calm, making decisive actions, and inspiring confidence amidst chaos.

- **Details:** "However, crises often come unannounced, catching us off guard and testing our limits. The pressure can be immense, and the path forward unclear."

3. Fuel the Journey

- **Journey:** The journey involves navigating through three key crises:

  1. **Crisis Story 1: The Financial Meltdown**
     - **Story:** Jane recounts the story of coaching a CFO during a major financial downturn. The company was on the brink of bankruptcy, and the CFO had to make tough decisions about layoffs and restructuring.
     - **Lesson:** The importance of transparent communication and quick, decisive actions.

  2. **Crisis Story 2: The Scandal**
     - **Story:** A CEO faced a massive PR crisis after a scandal involving key executives. Jane guided the CEO through restoring the company's reputation and rebuilding trust with stakeholders.
     - **Lesson:** Leading with integrity and taking responsibility.

  3. **Crisis Story 3: The Pandemic Pivot**
     - **Story:** During the COVID-19 pandemic, Jane helped a small business owner pivot their business model to adapt to the new normal, ensuring business continuity and employee safety.
     - **Lesson:** Innovation and flexibility in the face of unprecedented challenges.

4. Ignite the Transformation

- **Transformation:** The core message is that leaders can transform crises into opportunities for growth and innovation.

- **Insight:** "These stories illustrate that crises, while daunting, are also opportunities for leaders to step up, innovate, and inspire their teams. By staying calm, making strategic decisions, and leading with integrity, leaders can not only navigate through crises but emerge stronger."

5. Radiate the Resolution

- **Resolution:** Practical application of the lessons learned to future crises.
- **Application:** "By applying these principles, you can lead your teams through any crisis. Transparent communication, integrity, and innovation are your tools to turn challenges into victories."

6. Share the Spark

- **Action:** Encourage the audience to implement these insights in their own leadership practices.
- **Empowerment:** "As you leave today, think about how you can apply these lessons in your own leadership journey. Reflect on your current challenges and consider how you can turn them into opportunities for growth and innovation."

By following this Spark Storytelling Framework™, Jane Smith can craft a compelling and structured narrative that not only engages her audience but also provides them with valuable insights and practical tools for leading through crises. This example demonstrates how to take the elements of the framework and map them to a real-world presentation, making the content relatable and actionable for the audience.

Spark Steps

- Use the Spark Storytelling Framework™ to develop the narrative elements of your Radical Spark Signature Talk™.
- Check out the Spark Box at www.aleyaharris.com/spark-box for a downloadable version of the Spark Storytelling Framework™.

CHAPTER 21

Developing Your Radical Spark Signature Talk™ Outline

"Clarity is power. The more clear you are about what you want, the more likely you are to achieve it."
—Billy Cox

O nce you've crafted your narrative using the Spark Storytelling Framework™, it's time to seamlessly transition those elements into your Radical Spark Signature Talk™ outline. I designed this outline to help you construct a narrative-based presentation that captivates and maintains audience engagement, ensuring you shine as a thought leader your audience will be eager to connect with again.

The genesis of the Radical Spark Signature Talk™ Outline was organic, stemming from my quest to distill the essence of my most successful talks. I isolated the key components that consistently worked wonders by analyzing feedback from testimonials, speaker selection committees, and reflections on what resonated most in my speaking engagements. This outline synthesizes all those winning elements—from storytelling techniques to dynamic content and impactful calls to action.

With the Radical Spark Signature Talk™ Outline, you're not just putting together a presentation; you're crafting an experience. It balances stories, insights, and engagement so that the audience doesn't just listen—they participate. And when they participate, they remember. Follow this outline, and you can deliver not just a good presentation but an unforgettable one. Trust the process outlined in this book, and it's tough to go wrong. You're on your way to becoming a speaker who leaves a lasting impression.

The Radical Spark Signature Talk™ Outline

1. Kindle the Desire – Build the audience's emotional and intellectual desire for change or action. Talk about what they want more than anything related to your topic.

2. Illuminate the Challenge – Introduce the main challenge or problem your talk will address.

3. Describe the Steps of the Journey of Your Radical Spark Signature Talk™ – List the three key phases or milestones of the narrative journey you will take your audience on.

4. Articulate Your Controlling Idea – Clearly define your talk's central message or thesis that guides the narrative.

5. Present Your Lead Magnet (Flexible Placement) – Introduce a tool or resource that supports the talk's message (placement can vary based on the talk's flow).

6. Fuel the Journey with STEAM (Three Times) – Use the STEAM method to deepen the narrative.

   a. Story: Share relevant stories to illustrate your points.
   b. Teach: Provide educational content related to the stories.
   c. Experience: Engage the audience with immersive experiences inside of the room. Avoid experiences that cause dead air. You should be talking on stage, not waiting for the audience to complete an exercise.
   d. Action Step: Direct the audience on specific actions they can take.
   e. Main Idea: Reinforce the central theme or lesson of each section.

7. Reiterate Your Controlling Idea – Remind the audience of the core message and its relevance, especially now that you have articulated it more clearly throughout your presentation.

8. Closing Thought or Activity – End with a powerful closing that reinforces the talk's main message and leaves a lasting impression.

9. Share the Spark – Encourage the audience to spread the insights they've gained.

10. Reiterate Your Lead Magnet – Remind the audience of the lead magnet and its value.

11. Provide Your Contact Details with a Clear Call to Action – Offer clear next steps for the audience to engage further with you or your content.

The lead magnet and STEAM structure are the two elements of your outline that we haven't touched on so far.

A lead magnet is a valuable resource speakers offer to their audience in exchange for contact details, typically an email address. A lead magnet is a strategically developed resource offered to the audience to deepen engagement and extend the conversation beyond the presentation. This tool is crucial for building an email list and maintaining engagement with the audience after the presentation or event. Lead magnets provide quick wins. They relate to the presentation's topic or content, making them more relevant and interesting to a specific target audience. Lead magnets can take various forms, such as eBooks, quizzes, checklists, white papers, free consultations, or exclusive video content, each tailored to entice sign-ups and deepen the audience's engagement with the speaker or the brand.

Your lead magnet should complement and reinforce the messages and teachings delivered during your Radical Spark Signature Talk™. It is a tangible extension of the transformative journey initiated on stage, providing audience members with a valuable tool that supports their ongoing application of the insights gained. For instance, if the presentation's Controlling Idea revolves around improving communication skills, the lead magnet might be a comprehensive guide or video series that offers additional exercises and tips for enhancing these skills.

The lead magnet is strategically positioned within the Radical Spark Signature Talk™ Outline to support the talk's message. Introduce your lead magnet in the presentation where it can have the most impact, either as an incentive for further engagement or as a reinforcement of the commitment the audience has made by attending the talk. The placement ensures that the lead magnet serves as a resource and a reminder of the journey the audience has embarked on.

By integrating the lead magnet into this storytelling and presentation structure, speakers ensure that their message resonates beyond the confines of the event. This fosters ongoing engagement and enables audience members to more effectively implement the strategies and insights shared, ultimately enhancing the transformative impact of the talk.

STEAM is my favorite part of the outline because it keeps your presentation innately interesting. I also love it because I didn't plan the acronym; it just worked out perfectly. Don't you love it when life does that?

Let's break down each part of the STEAM Framework.

Story (S)

These are the stories you create using your Crisis Story Framework™. They connect you with the audience on an emotional level, illustrating key points or lessons through personal or relatable narratives.

For example, suppose your talk is about overcoming adversity. In that case, you might share a personal anecdote about a significant challenge you faced and how you overcame it, setting the stage for the lessons that follow.

Teach (T)

The Teach section is where you get to showcase your expertise. This portion focuses on the educational content of your presentation. It involves providing factual information, data, techniques, or methodologies related to the stories you share. Be careful to include information that is relevant to your Controlling Idea.

Following the story of overcoming adversity, you could teach the specific strategies or mindsets that are crucial for your audience to navigate through challenges based on the lessons in your story. Your teaching segment should provide insights that your audience can later turn into actions. Make sure to give tangible "how tos" that will enable your audience to take action.

Experience (E)

People can only listen to someone talk at them for a short amount of time before they start to check out mentally. In-presentation experiences allow your talk to become a two-way conversation where the audience transforms from passive listeners to active participants. Experiences also help your audience understand better or test out the tools you provide in the teaching section.

The key for the Experience portion is that there shouldn't be "dead air" on stage. This portion is not something your audience members are doing internally. You should continue to deliver a presentation as you invite the audience to participate. Unlike a workshop, you would not want them to take this time to write in a journal or talk to their neighbor about a discussion question.

Here are some examples of Experience formats:

- Group Chanting or Recitations: Involve the audience in group chants or recitations. You could use a motivational mantra related to the talk's theme, helping to energize the room and make the message memorable.
- Guided Visualization: Lead the audience through a guided visualization related to your talk's theme, helping them visualize success or achieving their goals.

- Repeat After Me: Get the audience to repeat key phrases or concepts after you. This tool reinforces important points and keeps the audience engaged and active.
- Live Polls: Use apps or tools to conduct live polls on audience opinions or choices about your topic. Share results in real time and discuss them briefly.
- Physical Activities: Engage the audience in simple physical activities like standing, stretching, or hand-raising to answer questions or "vote." This physical movement can help maintain energy levels in the room.

Action Step (A)

To reap the benefits of attending your session, audience members must take action based on your content. Otherwise, they will have wasted their time. The Action Step is about directing the audience on specific actions to implement the lessons learned. It's about moving from inspiration to action.

For example, you could challenge the audience to identify one personal or professional obstacle to which they can apply the taught strategies in the next week, encouraging immediate application of your teachings.

I also often use journal prompt questions for Action Steps.

Main Idea (M)

Each STEAM cycle culminates by reinforcing the central theme or lesson of the section, tying back to the Controlling Idea of the presentation. This is the classic "tell them what you are going to tell them, tell them, then tell them what you told them" situation. It is also great for signposting so the audience understands where you are in your presentation and what they should understand by that point.

When you create your outline, you write the exact words that belong on each slide so the slides are easier to build out later. But before we can get to the wording and structure, let's discuss how the narrative development work you've done translates to your outline.

CHAPTER 22

Mapping Your Story to Your Outline

"Marketing is no longer about the stuff that you make, but about the stories you tell."
—Seth Godin

So far, I've given you two tools to build the structure of your talk: The Spark Storytelling Framework™ and The Radical Spark Signature Talk™ Outline. Now, it's time to map the story-building work you've done into your outline so you know how to build out the specific content of each of your slides.

To effectively translate your Spark Storytelling Framework™ into the Radical Spark Signature Talk™ Outline, it's essential to understand how each element of the framework informs specific sections of the outline. This one-to-one mapping ensures a seamless transition from concept to structured presentation.

1. Kindle the Desire
- **Spark Storytelling Framework™:** Kindle the Desire
- **Radical Spark Signature Talk™ Outline:** Kindle the Desire

- Start by addressing what your audience yearns for concerning your topic. This emotional and intellectual appeal sets the stage for your entire presentation, making the audience feel invested.

2. Illuminate the Challenge

- **Spark Storytelling Framework™:** Illuminate the Challenge
- **Radical Spark Signature Talk™ Outline:** Illuminate the Challenge and Fuel the Journey (within STEAM)
    - Clearly define the problem that prevents the audience from achieving their desires. This foundational challenge sets up the stakes of your talk. Additionally, use this information to break down the main problem into three distinct parts within the STEAM sections, providing detailed stories, teachings, and actionable steps to address each aspect of the challenge.

3. Fuel the Journey

- **Spark Storytelling Framework™:** Fuel the Journey
- **Radical Spark Signature Talk™ Outline:** Describe the Steps of the Journey and Fuel the Journey (within STEAM)
    - Outline the key phases or milestones of the journey your audience will undertake. These steps match the STEAM sections of your outline, where you provide detailed stories, teachings, and experiences that guide the audience through the journey. Your crisis stories, successes, and gifts are integral to this journey, showing how each step helps resolve the challenge.

4. Ignite the Transformation

- **Spark Storytelling Framework™:** Ignite the Transformation

- **Radical Spark Signature Talk™ Outline:** Articulate Your Controlling Idea, Present Your Lead Magnet (both times), Reiterate Your Controlling Idea, and Fuel the Closing Thought or Activity
  - This element captures the core message or breakthrough insight that changes the audience's understanding or perspective. It forms the backbone of your Controlling Idea; you should reiterate it throughout your talk. Your lead magnet, designed to offer a quick win or first step towards transformation, ties into this concept. The closing thought or activity should solidify the transformation you've opened the audience up to.

5. Radiate the Resolution

- **Spark Storytelling Framework™:** Radiate the Resolution
- **Radical Spark Signature Talk™ Outline:** Fuel the Journey (within STEAM), Share the Spark, and Provide Your Contact with a Clear Call to Action
  - Demonstrate how your audience can apply their transformation in practical ways. Each STEAM section should provide a part of the overall resolution, helping the audience grasp how to move from point A to point B using your examples. Share the spark by encouraging the audience to implement what they've learned and ensure your contact information and call to action are presented to facilitate ongoing engagement.

6. Share the Spark

- **Spark Storytelling Framework™:** Share the Spark
- **Radical Spark Signature Talk™ Outline:** Share the Spark and Provide Your Audience with a Clear Call to Action

○ Empower the audience to take what they've learned and implement it in their lives. This final encouragement should resonate through your closing sections, offering a clear path for ongoing engagement and action.

Now that you know where each element of the Spark Storytelling Framework™ goes, you can build your Radical Spark Signature Talk™ Outline. The words you use in your outline should be the exact words you include on your slides. I like to create a simple bullet-pointed list, but you can use the template provided at the Spark Box to help you.

Spark Steps

- Use the Spark Storytelling Framework™ to create your Radical Spark Signature Talk™ Outline.
- Check out the Spark Box at www.aleyaharris.com/spark-box for a visual on how to map the Spark Storytelling Framework™ to your Radical Spark Signature Talk™ outline and to download a Radical Spark Signature Talk™ template.

CHAPTER 23

Creating Your Radical Spark Signature Talk™ Slides

"Visual storytelling of one kind or another has been around since cavemen were drawing on the walls."
—Frank Darabont

Congratulations! You've completed your Radical Spark Signature Talk™ Outline, and now it's time to bring your presentation to life visually. Moving from your outline to creating impactful slides is an essential step in crafting a compelling presentation that not only holds your audience's attention but also seamlessly guides them through your narrative journey.

Your slides are essential tools in your presentation arsenal, designed to support and enhance your performance on stage. They are not a crutch you rely on to remember what to say, nor are they there to overwhelm or distract your audience with excessive information. Instead, slides should be a visual aid that guides your audience through your narrative, reinforces your key points, and keeps them engaged throughout your talk.

Think of your slides as the backdrop to your story. Just as a great set design enhances a theatrical performance without overshadowing the actors, your slides should enhance your presentation without stealing the spotlight. They are there to support you, the speaker, by providing visual cues that highlight and emphasize your message.

You ensure they serve their role effectively by carefully crafting your slides with purpose and intention. Use them to clarify complex ideas, illustrate key points with visuals, and create a cohesive experience for your audience. Remember, the stars of the show are you and your story; the slides are simply there to help you shine.

In this section, we'll delve into the dos and don'ts of creating impactful slides, share key tips to keep your audience engaged, and ensure your visual aids complement your Radical Spark Signature Talk™ rather than detract from it.

Dos and Don'ts of Slide Creation

Creating effective slides is crucial for delivering a powerful Radical Spark Signature Talk™. Here are some essential dos and don'ts to guide you through the process, straight from my own experiences and lessons learned on stage.

Dos

1. Use Large, Legible Fonts
   ○ Ensure your text is big enough for everyone to read, whether in the front row or the nosebleed seats. Remember, they can't follow along if they can't read it. Go big or go home.

2. Stay On Brand
   - Keep your slides consistent with your brand's colors, fonts, and overall style. This will create a cohesive experience and reinforce your professional image. Consistency is key to looking polished and put together.

3. Limit Text
   - Aim for a maximum of seven words per slide. Yes, you read that right—seven. The fewer words, the better. Your slides are there to support your narrative, not to serve as a teleprompter. If it feels like you're cramming, you probably are. Break it up!

4. Use High-Quality Images
   - Invest in good visuals. Use relevant, high-quality images that enhance your message. Canva is a great tool for this, and I highly recommend upgrading to Canva Pro if you haven't already. And for the love of all that is good, avoid clip art like the plague.

5. Break Down Concepts
   - Spread out your ideas across multiple slides. Spacing out your text blocks makes your presentation more digestible and engaging. If you have a complex point, break it into smaller, easily understood chunks over several slides.

6. Have a General Theme for Imagery
   - Choose a theme for your visuals that complements your talk. Consistent imagery style helps maintain a professional look and feel. And no, cheesy 90s stock photos don't count as "consistent imagery."

7. Make Slides Photographable
    ○   Create slides that people will want to take pictures of. Think quotable, memorable, and shareable content. Subtly adding your logo at the bottom can also help build brand recognition as people snap and share your slides.

8. Leave Clues for Yourself
    ○   Use visual cues on your slides to help you stay on track. Whether it's a specific background for certain sections or little icons that only you know the meaning of, these clues can keep you from getting lost mid-presentation.

Don'ts

1. Avoid Overloading with Text
    ○   Don't fill your slides with paragraphs of text. Your audience should be listening to you, not reading a novel on the screen. Overloaded slides are a surefire way to lose their attention.

2. Skip the Fancy Fonts
    ○   Don't use overly fancy or hard-to-read fonts. They might look cool, but they're useless if they're not legible. Stick to clean, simple fonts that everyone can read without squinting. Keep accessibility in mind.

3. Steer Clear of Clip Art
    ○   Don't use outdated clip art. It's unprofessional and will make your presentation look stuck in a time warp. High-quality images are the way to go.

4. Ditch the Overly Posed Stock Photos
   ○ Don't use those cheesy, overly posed stock photos. They're not relatable and can make your presentation feel inauthentic. Opt for more natural, realistic images.

5. Avoid Heavy Dependence on Audio/Video
   ○ Don't rely heavily on audio or video files. Technical difficulties are the bane of any presenter's existence. If your tech setup isn't top-notch, it's best to avoid the potential pitfalls that audio and video bring.

6. Don't Write and Memorize Your Presentation
   ○ Don't write out and memorize your entire presentation. Your Radical Spark Signature Talk™ isn't a TEDx talk (that's a different format), and you're not a robot. Trust your outline, practice, and ability to engage with your audience more naturally and fluidly.

7. Don't Let Slide Count Intimidate You
   ○ Don't worry about the number of slides. Contrary to old-school norms, more slides can clarify your presentation by breaking down concepts. Just don't use it as an excuse to overload with content. Quality over quantity, folks.

By following these dos and don'ts, you'll create slides that support your Radical Spark Signature Talk™ and enhance your audience's overall experience. Remember, your slides are there to guide and reinforce your message, not to distract or overwhelm. Keep it clean, clear, and engaging.

Tips to Keep the Audience Engaged

Creating slides that complement your talk is crucial, but keeping your audience engaged goes beyond just visuals. Here are some tried-and-true tips to ensure your audience stays hooked from start to finish:

1. Be Authentic and Relatable
   Let your true self shine. Don't try to be someone you're not. Share personal stories and anecdotes that relate to your message. Authenticity is magnetic—it draws people in and keeps them interested.

   When I share my story about overcoming impostor syndrome in an abusive professional relationship, I'm not just talking about a problem; I'm sharing a part of my life that resonates with many. It makes me relatable and human.

2. Use Visual Cues and Clarity
   Use your slides to provide visual cues that help your audience follow along. It could be as simple as using consistent imagery for different sections or breaking up complex ideas over several slides.

   I like to use a specific background element for each part of the STEAM framework. It helps me stay on track and gives the audience a clear visual cue about where we are in the presentation.

3. Keep It Interactive
   Engage your audience with interactive elements. You could do anything from asking questions to having them perform

simple activities. Interaction breaks the monotony and makes your presentation more memorable.

During my talks, I often ask the audience to chant with me or participate in a quick exercise. It gets them involved and keeps the energy in the room high.

4. Show, Don't Just Tell
    Use visuals to show your points rather than just talking about them. Use images, diagrams, or short videos. Visual storytelling is powerful and helps drive your message home.

    Instead of just talking about the impact of a great leader, I show before-and-after scenarios with images and stories that highlight the transformation.

5. Keep Your Energy Up
    Your energy levels set the tone for the entire presentation. Be enthusiastic, animated, and passionate about your topic. If you're excited, your audience will be too.

    I bring my full energy to the stage, moving around, using my hands, and varying my voice to keep things dynamic. My enthusiasm is contagious, and it keeps the audience engaged.

6. Use Humor Wisely
    A well-placed joke or light-hearted comment can break the ice and make your audience feel more comfortable. Just make sure it's appropriate and relevant to your topic.

    I like to poke fun at myself and my past mistakes. It's a great way to connect with the audience and make them feel at ease.

7. Involve the Audience

   Make the audience part of your presentation. Ask for their input, have them share their experiences, or conduct live polls. This approach keeps the audience engaged and makes them feel valued.

   I often ask the audience to share their thoughts or experiences on a topic before I offer my own insights. This creates a dialogue rather than a monologue.

8. Keep It Simple

   Don't overwhelm your audience with too much information. Keep your slides simple and your points clear. Focus on delivering a few key messages effectively rather than cramming in everything you know.

   I try to stick to the seven words per slide rule and use clear, concise language. It helps the audience absorb the information without feeling overloaded.

9. Practice Makes Perfect

   Rehearse your presentation multiple times. Familiarity with your material will make you more confident and fluid on stage, allowing you to engage with the audience naturally.

   Before any major presentation, I practice in front of a mirror, record myself, and present to friends or family. Their feedback helps me refine my delivery and content.

10. Be Flexible

    Be prepared to adjust on the fly. Don't be afraid to pivot if something isn't working or the audience isn't responding as expected. Remember, you are a channel. Flexibility shows that you're in tune with your audience and can adapt to their needs.

If I notice the audience's energy dipping, I might switch up the order of my talk or throw in an unexpected interactive element to re-engage them. I also take a second to tap into Spirit.

Creating your Radical Spark Signature Talk™ slides is about more than just putting words on a screen. It's about enhancing your storytelling, keeping your audience engaged, and ensuring you deliver your message with clarity and impact. You create a cohesive and engaging presentation by using large, legible fonts, maintaining consistency in your visual themes, and incorporating storytelling elements and visual metaphors. Highlighting key data points and practicing with your slides ensures a seamless delivery that keeps your audience focused on your message. Remember, your slides are tools to support your performance on stage, not to overshadow it. Keep them simple, clear, and visually appealing, and you'll create a powerful presentation that resonates with your audience and leaves a lasting impression.

CHAPTER 24

Clarity Achieved: The Core of Your Message

"A moment of clarity without any action is just a thought that passes in the wind. But a moment of clarity followed by an action is a pivotal moment in our life."
—Don Miguel Ruiz Jr.

As we conclude Section 2: Get Clear, take a moment to appreciate your progress. You've delved deep into your personal stories, crafted your Crisis Stories, and started to build a cohesive narrative that resonates with your authentic self. This clarity is the foundation of your Radical Spark Signature Talk™. It's what makes your message compelling and your delivery powerful.

In this section, you've learned how to effectively utilize the Crisis Story Framework™, develop Success Celebrations, gather your unique gifts, and identify your Golden Thread. Each element has helped you build a cohesive, impactful narrative that aligns with your core message and engages your audience from start to finish.

As you move forward, keep refining your stories and stay true to your authentic self. The clarity you've achieved here is just the

171

beginning. With a strong foundation, you're ready to take your speaking to the next level.

Spark Steps

- Develop your Crisis Stories using the Crisis Story Framework™.
- Create your lists of successes and gifts and roll them into your Crisis Stories. Also, keep them handy for a confidence boost.
- Create your Golden Thread and Controlling Idea for your Radical Spark Signature Talk™.
- Use the Spark Storytelling Framework™ to build out the narrative of your Radical Spark Signature Talk™.
- Create your Radical Spark Signature Talk™ Outline.
- Create your Radical Spark Signature Talk™ Slides.
- Give yourself a huge congratulations because you just did a lot of heavy lifting!
- Check out the Spark Box at www.aleyaharris.com/spark-box for tools to help you get clear.
- Get Clear is often the most challenging section for many of my Spark the Stage™ students. Luckily, they have support from me and their fellow students to ask questions, get feedback on their outlines, and feel confident that their Radical Spark Signature Talk™ makes sense. If you want to move more seamlessly from story to stage, sign up for the Spark the Stage course at www.aleyaharris.com/spark.

Section 3
Get Connected

"'Cause if it don't make dollars, it don't make sense."
—DJ Quik

R adically Authentic Strategic Storytelling™ Authentic Strategic Storytelling extends beyond the presentation contents to the stage and how you make money as a professional speaker. In this section, we will talk about how to bring your Radical Spark Signature Talk™ to life and how to make it make sense for your bank account.

In this section, we will connect you to your audience and you to your money.

CHAPTER 25

Use Your Tools to Master the Stage

**"All the tools, techniques and technology in the world are
nothing without the head, heart and hands to use them wisely,
kindly and mindfully."**
—Rasheed Ogunlaru

As we move into the stagecraft piece of this book, I
want to draw your attention back to the definition of a
professional speaker.

*A professional speaker is a performance artist who makes money
by clearly communicating helpful ideas from the stage, virtually or
in person.*

Please note the "performance artist" piece. That is what we're
talking about now—performing. If I were an audience member
and wanted to read a blog post about what you were talking about,
I would just read the blog post. I don't need you to read it to me; I
need you to perform the words. Act out the story. Show me, engage
me, and make me feel something.

In addition to the slides on the screen and your content,
your tools are your body, the stage, your voice, and the audience
themselves. All four things will make you more compelling when
you use them correctly. Use every part of yourself to communicate,

including your words, energy, tone, and body. All of your tools help articulate your Controlling Idea and your main points so your audience can reach the transformation they need and you can serve them as much as possible.

Your Body

Your body is one of your best illustrative tools. By changing where your body is in space and thinking of how you can use it in a 360-degree fashion, you can become more dynamic on stage. Using your knees to get low, turning your back to the audience for a moment, and stretching your arms out from side to side are great ways to illustrate your message and unpack your Controlling Idea.

Here are a few of my favorite tips for using your body on stage like a pro:

- Soften your knees so you don't look like a robot. A slight bend will help your movements appear more natural, allowing you to move more gracefully and fluidly across the stage.

- Remember that your body includes your fingertips and your toes. Extend your arms, use your feet, and articulate through your body like a dancer.

- Match your movements to your stories and your voice. If you're talking about something grandiose, you want to have big arms stretching out, reaching up, reaching out to the sky. If you're bringing the presentation to a more emotional place, you might have your hands on your heart, close to your chest, or on your stomach.

- Don't shy away from bringing the drama. You're really just one beat away from dancing on that stage. You're constantly moving, filling the stage with your energy. Do not be afraid to take up space.

- Use commonly understood body language for your benefit. Practice posing in the mirror to see what your body language communicates. How will your audience perceive you if you cross your arms, put your hands on your hips, throw your arms up in the air, or stand with your legs far apart? Don't resign yourself to just standing and shuffling behind a microphone. It's not fun to do, and it's not fun to look at.

The Stage

To best use the stage, think in 3D. Speakers commonly move from the left to the right and often forget to move forward and backward. Moving further away from your audience creates a feeling of separation, depth, or expansion. Imagine stepping further and further toward the back of the stage as you spoke about how each step you took to solve your problem took you further from your goal. That connection between your movement and your words paints a picture that helps the audience better comprehend your point and empathize with your feelings.

As you consider moving backward on the stage, make sure to find and stay in your light (the physical light and the Light from your Spirit). At the back of most stages, the light often drops off, and you will just look like a shadow. Standing in the shadows robs you of the connection with your audience, is distracting, and will make any photos or videos come out less than ideal.

Moving forward on the stage can illustrate similar points to moving backward. When you move as far forward as possible, you will encounter a place most speakers don't think to use but where a bit of magic happens: the stage's edge. At the stage's edge is an invisible wall between you and the audience. Often, this is the barrier between the "sage on stage" and the "plebs in the seats." However, I encourage you to be the speaker leading a group experience, not someone seeking to feed their ego with the spotlight. What would happen if you leaned in and broke through the invisible barrier (safely)? You could engage and connect with your audience to show you are all in it together. Breaking the barrier also captures your audience's attention and makes your presentation more dynamic.

While I encourage you to lean forward while on the stage, I do not encourage you to leave. Speakers leave the stage and don't use a mic because they think it makes them appear to be "just one of the people" when, in reality, it makes it difficult to hear and see them. The audience wastes their brain power on searching for the speaker rather than focusing on the content and how it relates to their life experience. Also, people came to listen to an empathetic leader. By getting off the stage, you diminish their investment of time and money.

If movement on stage doesn't come easily to you, use the "five slide switch" rule. Every five slides, slowly move your way over to the other side of the stage. Click through five more slides, then slowly move to the other side of the stage. That way, you are still moving. If it's not natural for you to move, you at least know you're keeping people's interest during your presentation by moving your body in space in a more structured way.

Your Voice

Since I am a speaker and podcast host, I love using and modulating my voice. Think about where your voice is coming from in your body. When you speak from your diaphragm, your voice will boom. Pushing air out through your nose and focusing your voice through your face may sound more high-pitched. When I think about how to best match my voice and tone to the needs of the presentation, I employ my old vocal training and become intentional with how I use my tongue, throat, lungs, and mouth to vary the listening experience for the audience, so they stay engaged and better understand the content.

If you are getting easily short of breath, I recommend doing breathing exercises like a singer would to increase your lung capacity. You could also try hot yoga (again, a personal fav) or aerobics. Make most of your presentation come from your diaphragm, not your throat, so you don't speak yourself hoarse. If you find yourself shouting, ask the AV person to turn up your mic. Always use a mic. If the room has two people or 2,000 people, use a mic.

The Audience

Point at people. Wave to people. Talk about one side of the room to the other side of the room "behind their backs." Use the people in the audience as engagement tools. When you do that, it takes a big experience and makes it feel more engaging and personal.

If the room is small enough (most likely less than 500 people), ask for three names of folks in the front few rows at the beginning of your presentation and use them throughout. I usually say something like, "Hey, what's your name? Jerri? You seem like a cool cat, Jerri. Loving the hat." Then, when I talk about a point later in the presentation, I could say something like, "Well, we can't all have cool hats like Jerri, but I do try to look my best." Connecting directly with a few people makes the whole room feel connected. The key is always to be complementary and never disparage anyone. Be careful of even good-natured teasing that someone could perceive as bullying.

I also employ the classic "raise your hand if" technique to encourage group participation and to break the steady drumbeat of my voice. Always ask the audience to raise their hands for something that will make them look good or neutral if others see their hands raised. For example, "Raise your hand if you would love to get a million dollars right now, no strings attached" is excellent. "Raise your hand if you're deeply in debt" is not OK. Always validate, always encourage. Say things like, "Oh, my gosh, you guys are so smart. You raised your hand, and you knew that. I didn't know that until last year. Let me tell you a story of how I learned that."

Before the presentation starts, I mingle with the organizers and the people in the room, and I ask them things like, "What have you all been up to so far in this conference?" Or "What are you planning on doing next?" Or "What's been your favorite part of this conference so far?" I'm gathering intel, and I use that intel on the stage. The more personal you can make an experience, even if you haven't edited your slides with that personalization, the better your presentation will go.

Control the Experience from the Moment You Enter the Room

Depending on the event, manage the energy of the room from the moment you enter it until the moment you leave. I encourage you to start with a grand entrance. Plan the music as you will walk up the stage. It hypes you up and hypes up the audience. I provide the song that I want to have played, and it allows the vibe to change before I even open my mouth. Controlling the transition into your stage experience means it doesn't matter what the speaker before you did, how good they were, or how their content landed. You get to reset the room. You control the energy, and you control the stage.

Your grand entrance could be small, like choosing a great song, or grandiose, like being carried in on a litter like an Egyptian queen or employing acrobats and jugglers. How creative you get depends on the event, your budget, your brand, and your content. Dare to be different.

Spark Steps

- Assess Your Stage Presence: Take some time to reflect on your current stage presence. How comfortable are you moving around the stage? Do you feel your body language is expressive and aligned with your message? Identify areas for improvement and set goals for enhancing your stage presence.
- Practice Dynamic Movement: Find a space to move freely and practice your presentation. Focus on using your body to illustrate your points. Incorporate movements like bending your knees, extending your arms, and shifting your position on the stage. Record yourself, if possible, to review and adjust your movements for maximum impact.
- Experiment with Voice Modulation: Record yourself reading a section of your presentation. Play with different vocal tones, pitches, and volumes to see how they change the delivery of your message. Practice speaking from your diaphragm to project your voice clearly and confidently.
- Engage with the Audience: Plan interactive elements to incorporate into your presentation. Think about how you can involve the audience, whether by asking questions, using names, or encouraging group participation. Practice these interactions to ensure they feel natural and engaging.
- Control the Room's Energy: Decide on an entrance strategy that aligns with your brand and content. Choose a song or create a grand entrance that sets the tone for your presentation.

Practice your entrance to ensure it flows smoothly and captures the audience's attention from the start.

- Inside of my Spark the Stage™ course, I show students exactly how to move their bodies on stage. They even get a chance to ask questions and submit videos for review. If you would like more support on how to stand in your power in front of an audience, sign up for Spark the Stage™ at www.aleyaharris. com/spark.

CHAPTER 26

Get the Gig

"There is no monopoly on becoming a millionaire. If you're jealous of those with more money, don't just sit there and complain—do something to make more money yourself."
—Gina Rinehart

Mmm, yeah, baby. Now we're getting to the good stuff. The rest of this book is all about making money, honey. We will connect your passion, the audience's problem, and your paycheck into a lovely and lucrative relationship. Remember, we are professional speakers, and professionals make money. We will start by helping you decide how much money you want to make and the goals you want to set.

You may be asking yourself, "We are doing this now? Why wasn't goal setting at the beginning of the book?" At the beginning of the book, you were asking yourself questions like, "Do I have anything to say? Will people want to hear it?" and you would have set your goals too low. You would have been way too open to underselling yourself. By now, you hopefully realize how valuable you and your message are and are primed to set loftier goals. You also have probably refined how speaking will help support other areas of your business, and you may have even contemplated making tweaks to your company because of the direction of your

Radical Spark Signature Talk ™. You are now in a better mind space to define how you would like abundance to flow to you.

Goal Setting

> *"Intentions compressed into words enfold magical power."*
> —Deepak Chopra

One of the key elements of a successful speaking career is setting clear, achievable goals. This may sound like common sense, but it's an area where many speakers falter. Setting goals isn't just about knowing what you want; it's about creating a roadmap that helps you get there. Let's dive into the practicalities of setting and achieving your goals as a professional speaker.

My first question to you is simple: How much money do you want to make?

Your immediate response might be, "As much as humanly possible. Duh!" But I want you to dig a little deeper. What is the job or purpose of this speaking revenue stream? Is it meant to replace your income or simply provide supplementary income? Would you simply like an extra $10,000 per year to go on a family vacation, or are you trying to develop a six-figure speaking business? Let's give the money a job.

Your goal for using the money will determine how much you need to make. It will also provide parameters for the events you apply to, how frequently you apply, and how much money you are willing to invest in becoming a professional speaker. You will feel empowered to make better decisions in your business when you are clear about how speaking fits into your revenue generation plan. For example, if you're only trying to make $10,000 a year from speaking, you would not necessarily allocate all of your marketing budget to acquiring paid speaking engagements and instead make sure to invest in other activities to attract new clients.

Once you know how much money you want to make and how you will use it, I want you to ask yourself how frequently you want to travel. Professional speakers who make most of their revenue from being on stages are also on planes very often, sometimes weekly or more. You could decide that a lot of travel is a horrible or wonderful fit for your lifestyle. You could decide to speak globally, locally, or only virtually. You are in control and get to shape your speaking career around your other priorities like your family and hobbies. How often you want to travel will determine the types of calls for speakers you apply to.

My third question is, "How many years do you want to be a professional speaker?" Your response could be as extended as you desire, but it will change how you approach your career. I have a secret (don't tell anybody): I don't want to be a professional speaker forever. Traveling, being away from my little girl, feeling burnout, constantly refreshing to avoid getting stale and irrelevant… I will eventually phase out speaking as my primary revenue stream (at least, that's what I think right now).

Also, I have bigger plans. My vision is to be "Oprah Big," and focusing on speaking rather than my larger thought leadership platform will hinder my progress. I want to take my speaker money and invest it into real estate, other companies, and to build up my community. The way I am structuring my speaking career is to enable my larger vision. How do your larger vision and current priorities inform the length of your career?

My final question is, "What is your speaking zenith?" What does the top look like for you? Is it delivering a TEDx talk? Is it talking to a stadium full of 30,000 people? Your speaking zenith could be closely related to your Ideal Scene. Start with the highest point in mind and work backward from there. For example, if your zenith is to deliver a keynote in Germany, align your message with your ideal German customer. Determine what companies and conferences have a presence in Germany. Start reaching out to German contacts on LinkedIn to build rapport.

Base your decisions on how you move forward with marketing yourself and the type of Radical Spark Signature Talk™ on your answers to these questions. Take your time to answer them and lean into points of discomfort. If you feel unclear, ask complementary questions to get to the root of the issue. Use goal setting to set yourself up for success.

Manifesting Your Speaking Gigs

> *"The entire universe is conspiring*
> *to give you everything that you want."*
> —*Abraham-Hicks*

Setting goals and taking action are vital to securing speaking gigs, but they are only part of the equation. To truly harness the power of the universe and attract the opportunities you desire, you must embrace the principles of manifestation. Drawing inspiration from the teachings of greats like Deepak Chopra, *The Secret*, and Abraham-Hicks, we'll explore how to use manifestation techniques to get the gigs you want.

Manifestation is the process of turning your dreams into reality through the power of thought, intention, and action. It's about aligning your energy with the opportunities you seek and inviting them into your life. Here's how you can leverage manifestation to secure speaking gigs:

Manifestation isn't just about wishful thinking; it's a deliberate practice that involves several key principles:

- Clear Intention: Be specific about what you want. The universe responds to clarity. Write down your goals and visualize them as already achieved.
- Belief: Believe that you deserve and can achieve your goals. Doubt creates resistance.
- Positive Emotion: Feel the emotions of having already achieved your goals. Joy, gratitude, and excitement amplify your manifestation power.
- Action: While manifestation involves the power of thought and intention, it also requires taking inspired action. Move towards your goals with confidence and determination.

The Ideal Scene Essence Expedition you completed earlier is a powerful tool for manifestation. By vividly imagining your ideal speaking scenarios and feeling the emotions associated with those experiences, you align yourself with the energy of success. Regularly revisit your Ideal Scenes, adding details and deepening your emotional connection to them. This practice helps solidify your vision and attracts similar opportunities into your reality.

Maintaining a positive and clear mindset is crucial for successful manifestation. Here are some tips to help you stay aligned with your goals:

- Affirmations: Use positive affirmations to reinforce your goals and beliefs. Statements like "I am a sought-after speaker who captivates and inspires audiences" can help shift your mindset.
- Gratitude: Practice gratitude daily. Focus on what you have and what you've achieved, and express thanks for the opportunities coming your way.
- Visualization: Regularly visualize your Ideal Scenes and feel the emotions associated with them. Imagine yourself on stage, delivering impactful talks and receiving positive feedback.

- Stay Positive: Keep your thoughts positive and avoid dwelling on setbacks or negative outcomes. Abraham-Hicks teaches, "What you think about activates a vibration within you." Stay focused on your desires, not your doubts.

Integrating these manifestation techniques into your routine will create a powerful synergy between your goals, intentions, and actions. This alignment will help you attract your desired speaking gigs and amplify your impact as a professional speaker. Embrace the process, stay positive, and watch as the opportunities you've envisioned materialize.

Spark Steps

- Write down the answers to the following questions to set your professional speaking goals:
    - How much money do you want to make?
    - What is that job of the money you make from being a professional speaker?
    - How frequently do you want to travel?
    - How many years do you want to be a professional speaker?
    - What is your ultimate career vision?
    - What is your speaking zenith?
- Revisit Your Ideal Scene Essence Expedition.
- Set Clear Intentions. Be precise about the types of gigs, audiences, and outcomes you desire.

- Create positive affirmations about your speaking goals and repeat them daily to reinforce your beliefs and intentions.
- Keep a gratitude journal to express thanks for what you have and the opportunities coming your way.
- Reflect on your achievements and express gratitude for future speaking gigs as if they are already secured.
- Still not feeling confident that you are a budding radically authentic professional speaker? Head over to the Spark Box at www.aleyaharris.com/spark-box and listen to my confidence meditation. You can also join Spark the Stage ™ to get the clarity, confidence boost, and community you need to bring your ideas to life. Sign up at www.aleyaharris.com/spark.

CHAPTER 27

Put Yourself in a Box

"Be who you are and say what you feel because those who mind don't matter and those who matter don't mind."
—Dr. Seuss

I know that your mother told you that you are super special, and I agree with her. However, to help others understand your specialness, you must put yourself in a box. Your box has packaging that you craft specifically for you. The packaging helps people understand you, manage their expectations for what's inside, and determine if having the box will solve whatever problem they are dealing with. You need to craft your package to match your ideal customer's perception.

If you want to be the speaker who is on stage in front of 2,000 corporate executives, you need to put yourself in a box that matches that expectation. That could look like a polished brand image, clear messaging, and a slick website with flashy videos of you speaking. On the other hand, if you're trying to become an individual retreat speaker to small groups of 10 to 20 soul-seekers, you might have a more flowy vibe. You may still be polished but less corporate. Your messaging might be more relaxed, friendly, and woo.

In this section, I will walk you through developing your speaker package to meet your goals. We will focus on your unique value proposition (UVP), brand, and niche to do that. Think of those three things like what people expect from your box, how people recognize your box, and what type of people will be raving fans of your box.

For example, the contents of my box include Radically Authentic Strategic Storytelling™, my on-stage presence, my experience as a marketer, and my energy. Those things differentiate me and are rooted in my purpose: to love people into the highest versions of themselves at scale. When I come into a room, not many people have that same mix of fabulousness, which makes me stand out. My uniqueness also matches the value I promise: I will be telling and helping other people tell radically authentic stories. I also promise that people will feel good and be edutained (educated + entertained).

When people buy my box, they know what to expect because I also maintain a consistent look. The outside of my box is super cute. I always have some type of fuschia in my lipstick, dress, or shoes, and I have big and curly hair. I always wear one of my brand colors and dress relatively conservatively (with a pinch of sass). I package myself the same way every time so that audiences know what to expect and so that I am recognizable as a "product."

If you were going to go to the store and buy some cough medicine, let's say it's Robitussin, and every time you went, the box looked different, you wouldn't be able to recognize that it was Robitussin. You might also start to feel a sense of distrust. You would not be as loyal, even if Robitussin were the best cough syrup out there, because the brand wasn't loyal to your expectations. Packaging yourself consistently and presenting a consistent message helps you solidify your differentiated position and build trust.

Now, my box is not for everyone. After a recent speaking engagement, I received survey feedback: "Alas, I am not a fan of Sanskrit chanting nor the idea of being a witchy spell-casting communicator. This presentation took a sharp left turn 1/3 of the way through and I could not get back on board with the material." Ahh… music to my ears! Why? Because that means I wasn't that person's person, and that is more than OK.

While they were feeling unattracted to me, most of that session left comments like, "Her energy alone is magnificent. Her knowledge and tips she provided are life changing for me and speak to my new upcoming role as a leader." To that I say, "Hi, new friend!" I got booked to speak by that group or people from it twice and counting. A good box will repel the folks that are not for you and attract the ones who are.

If I were to articulate what people expect from my box, my unique value proposition (UVP), it would be "Energetically facilitating the transformation of organizations and individuals through Radically Authentic Strategic Storytelling™ for lasting impact." When a conference organizer, event planner, or association books me, they know exactly what they are getting. I even summed it up in my tagline, "Aleya Harris is the Spark for Your Spark™."

A unique value proposition is the specific and differentiated solution that you provide and the promise of value that audiences can expect.

Here are a few examples:

- Leadership & Motivational Speaker: Jamal Smith inspires leaders to embrace authentic leadership through vulnerability and resilience, transforming organizations by building cohesive and motivated teams.
- Health & Wellness Speaker: Dr. Paula Vasquez revolutionizes personal wellness by bridging the gap between modern science and holistic practices, offering transformative insights for optimal health.

- Technology & Innovation Speaker: Sarah Li demystifies the future of technology, making complex concepts accessible and engaging and inspiring audiences to embrace innovation and drive progress within their organizations.

If you are the kind of person who likes a framework for your UVP, you could use:

"I help [Target Audience] achieve [Benefit/Outcome] through [Unique Solution], leveraging my [Key Differentiators] to ensure [Impact/Value]."

If I were to use that framework, my UVP would sound like "I help corporate leaders and teams achieve enhanced communication and performance through engaging keynotes on Radically Authentic Strategic Storytelling™, leveraging my years of experience as a marketer and dynamic on-stage presence to ensure lasting impact and increased team cohesion."

Once you've crafted your UVP, it's crucial to weave it into every aspect of your professional presence. Even if the exact wording doesn't show up on your website (although it could), your UVP's essence should be the guide for your speaker box. Every presentation, workshop, and piece of content you create should reflect the essence of your UVP, reinforcing your unique strengths and the specific benefits you offer. By consistently communicating your UVP, you build trust and recognition with your audience, setting a clear and compelling expectation for the transformative experience you provide.

Your UVP helps inform your brand. Your brand is, according to Jeff Bezos, "what other people say about you when you are not in the room." Think of your brand as the legacy you leave behind, the story people tell about you. When crafting your story, it's essential to be intentional about your actions, the products you offer, and the topics you discuss because all of these elements shape your legacy and brand.

I'm very intentional about focusing on Radically Authentic Strategic Storytelling™. Everything I share, whether online or in person, aligns with this core message. It's not just about talking the talk; it's about walking the walk. When you catch me at a conference, you'll see me taking the time to genuinely connect with people because I care deeply about helping others reach their highest potential.

To effectively communicate your brand, create a one-liner that encapsulates your UVP. A one-liner is your answer to the question, "What do you do?" It combines the problem you solve, your unique solution, and the result your audience achieves. For example, my one-liner is: "Don't let communication breakdowns, toxic environments, and disengaged employees rob your innovation and productivity. Aleya Harris helps business leaders overcome communication and differentiation challenges by sharing radically authentic stories that transform workplace culture and carve unique market niches." This format ensures that your brand is clear, compelling, and memorable, leaving a lasting impression on those who encounter it.

If we were to create one-liners from the UVP examples above, they would be:

- Leadership & Motivational Speaker: Don't let disengagement and lack of inspiration hold your team back. Jamal Smith empowers leaders with authentic storytelling and visionary leadership principles, transforming teams through motivation and engagement.
- Health & Wellness Speaker: Don't let unhealthy habits and lack of motivation compromise your well-being. Dr. Paula Vasquez promotes holistic wellness with evidence-based

practices and motivational lifestyle changes, guiding you to vibrant health and lasting vitality.

- Technology & Innovation Speaker: Don't let outdated technology hinder your business growth. Sarah Li drives success with cutting-edge technological insights and innovative solutions, helping you stay ahead in a rapidly evolving digital landscape.

As you develop your unique value proposition (UVP) and brand, it's crucial to identify and understand your ideal customers. This step ensures that your efforts are targeted and effective, allowing you to resonate deeply with those who will benefit most from your message. The key to a successful speaking career lies in recognizing that not everyone will be your customer, and that's perfectly OK.

Imagine trying to cater to everyone—it's like trying to sell water to a fish. You need to narrow down your audience to those who genuinely need and appreciate what you offer. This approach not only saves you time and resources but also helps you craft a message that speaks directly to your audience's hearts.

Let's delve into the process of identifying your ideal customers. Firstly, consider the specific problems your ideal customer faces and how your unique solution addresses these problems. For instance, if you are a leadership and motivational speaker, your ideal customer might be executives and managers struggling with employee engagement and organizational change. Your UVP would center around providing strategies and inspiration to help them lead more effectively.

One of the biggest fears when niching down is that you might exclude potential clients. However, if you try to sell to everyone, you will sell to no one. It's essential to narrow your focus to a specific group that you can serve exceptionally well. For example, rather than targeting all female business owners, you might focus on female engineers who are transitioning into leadership roles. This specificity allows you to hone your messaging and offer solutions tailored to their unique challenges.

To find your ideal customers, start by looking at the census data for your local area or industry-specific statistics. This research can provide valuable insights into the size and characteristics of your potential market. For instance, if you are targeting female civil engineers, you can find out how many there are in your area or industry and what their common challenges are.

Once you have identified your niche, refine your messaging to address their specific needs and desires. Messaging directed at a broad audience tends to be generic and bland. On the other hand, a targeted message speaks directly to the unique problems and aspirations of your ideal customer, making it more impactful and engaging.

If you're unsure about who your ideal customers are, start with what you know and enjoy. Reflect on your past experiences and passions. When I transitioned into the wedding catering and events industry after being laid off in February 2020, I did so because I enjoyed it and had a background as a chef. This industry alignment helped me find joy and success in my work. Similarly, think about what brings you joy and who you would love to serve. Start there, and be open to evolving as you gain more clarity and experience.

Entrepreneurship is a journey of constant evolution. Take inspiration from Beyoncé, who has continually reinvented herself while maintaining a core essence. She started with R&B, transitioned to celebrating African culture, moved to a Renaissance vibe, and now explores country music. Her ability to keep her brand fresh while staying true to her core identity keeps her audience engaged. As a speaker and entrepreneur, you have the freedom to evolve and adapt, but you need to start with a specific focus.

Niching down can make your marketing efforts more effective and less overwhelming. For instance, if you decide to focus on the cannabis industry, you can start by researching cannabis industry conferences, associations, and top companies. This targeted approach makes it easier to find and connect with your ideal customers. Use tools like LinkedIn Sales Navigator to dive deeper into the industry and build your network.

While it's tempting to cast a wide net, remember that specificity leads to clarity and connection. Define your niche by industry and demographics, such as women entrepreneurs aged 25 to 35 in Los Angeles with businesses generating $1 to 5 million in revenue. These criteria are easily searchable and provide a clear target for your marketing efforts.

Psychographic niching, which focuses on attitudes, interests, and values, can be more challenging but also rewarding. For example, targeting individuals passionate about personal growth requires a different approach than targeting based on demographics alone. However, when starting out, it's often easier to begin with industry and demographic niches.

Defining your ideal customers allows you to craft a message that resonates deeply with those you aim to serve. By understanding their unique challenges and desires, you can position yourself as the solution they've been looking for. Go forth, define your niche, and watch your speaking career flourish as you connect with the right people who value your unique contributions.

To develop your ideal customer and niche, find the answers to these questions:

1. Demographics
    ○   Age Range: What is the age range of your ideal customer?
    ○   Gender: Are they primarily male, female, or a mix?
    ○   Location: Where do they live? (City, state, region)

- Education Level: What is their highest level of education?
- Income Level: What is their income range?
- Marital Status: Are they single, married, divorced, etc.?
- Family Size: Do they have children? If so, how many?

2. Professional Information
   - Industry: What industry do they work in?
   - Job Title: What is their job title or role?
   - Work Experience: How many years of experience do they have?
   - Company Size: Do they work in a small, medium, or large company?
   - Career Goals: What are their professional aspirations?

3. Psychographics
   - Interests: What are their hobbies and interests?
   - Values: What values are important to them?
   - Lifestyle: What kind of lifestyle do they lead? (Active, health-conscious, family-oriented, etc.)
   - Attitudes: What are their attitudes towards work, life, and personal growth?
   - Challenges: What are their biggest pain points or challenges?
   - Motivations: What motivates them to take action or make decisions?

4. Behavioral Information
   - Buying Habits: How do they prefer to make purchases? (Online, in-store, both)
   - Brand Loyalty: Are they loyal to specific brands or open to trying new ones?

- Decision-Making Process: How do they make decisions? (Quickly, after thorough research, based on recommendations)
- Preferred Communication Channels: How do they prefer to receive information? (Email, social media, phone, in-person)
- Event Attendance: Do they attend industry conferences, webinars, workshops, etc.?

5. Specific Needs and Desires
   - Primary Goals: What are their main goals or aspirations related to your topic?
   - Specific Problems: What specific problems do they face that your talk can address?
   - Desired Outcomes: What outcomes are they seeking from your talk or services?
   - Preferred Solutions: What types of solutions do they prefer? (Practical tips, inspirational stories, strategic advice)

6. Examples and Case Studies
   - Success Stories: Can you identify past clients or audience members who fit this profile?
   - Testimonials: What have past clients said about your work that can help refine this profile?
   - Common Traits: What common traits do your most satisfied clients share?

By answering these questions, you can create a detailed and specific profile of your ideal customer, which will help you tailor your message and marketing efforts to resonate with them deeply.

By now, you should have a clearer picture of what it means to put yourself in a box and why it's essential for your speaking success. We've explored your Unique Value Proposition (UVP), discussed the importance of your brand, and helped you identify your ideal customer. This process might feel a bit restrictive at first, but it's actually about honing in on what makes you, you, and showcasing that to the world in the most effective way possible.

Your UVP is your promise to your audience, setting the expectation for the unique benefits only you can deliver. Your brand is the perception others have of you when you're not in the room—it's your legacy. Your ideal customer profile ensures you're speaking directly to those who will benefit most from your message, making your marketing efforts more targeted and effective.

Think of these elements as the foundational pillars of your speaking career. They work together to create a cohesive, compelling narrative that attracts the right opportunities and helps you stand out in a crowded market. By putting yourself in a box, you're not limiting yourself; you're providing a clear, recognizable, and memorable experience that your audience can trust and connect with.

As you move forward, remember that this "box" isn't a rigid container but a dynamic framework that evolves as you grow. Stay true to your core values and unique qualities while being open to new opportunities and adjustments along the way. Your UVP, brand, and ideal customer profile will guide your journey, helping you build a thriving speaking career that reflects your true self and resonates deeply with your audience.

Spark Steps

Define Your Unique Value Proposition (UVP):

- Reflect on your unique qualities, experiences, and skills.
- Write a UVP statement that communicates the specific value you provide and the promise of that value to your audience.
- Use the UVP template: "I help [Ideal Customer] achieve [Desired Outcome] by providing [Unique Solution/Approach]."

Craft Your Brand Identity:

- Think about what you want people to say about you when you're not in the room.
- List your core values and how they translate into your work as a speaker.
- Develop a consistent look and feel for your brand, including your visual identity (colors, fonts, logos) and your personal style (attire, presentation).
- Ensure all your communication (website, social media, marketing materials) aligns with your brand identity.

Identify Your Ideal Customer:

- Describe your ideal customer using demographics (age, gender, location, industry) and psychographics (interests, values, pain points).
- Consider who you enjoy working with and who will benefit most from your message.

- Create a detailed ideal customer profile to guide your marketing efforts and speaking engagements.

Create Your One-Liner:

- Develop a concise one-liner that answers the question, "What do you do?" by combining the problem you solve, your unique solution, and the result your audience receives.
- Example structure: "I help [Ideal Customer] overcome [Problem] by providing [Unique Solution] that [Results/Benefits]."

Integrate Your UVP, Brand, and Ideal Customer into Your Marketing Materials:

- Update your website, social media profiles, and marketing materials to reflect your UVP, brand, and ideal customer profile.
- Use your one-liner in your bios, introductions, and pitches to ensure consistency and clarity.

Test and Refine:

- Engage with your audience and collect feedback on your UVP, brand, and messaging.
- Make adjustments as needed to ensure you are resonating with your ideal customer and effectively communicating your value.

Need help to know if you are doing it right? You should start by using your Radically Authentic Self as your guide. If you are still unsure, head to the Spark Box at www.aleyaharris.com/spark-box to schedule a call with me. I can use my 15+ years as a marketer and strategist to help you feel confident that you are on track.

You can also sign up for Spark the Stage™ at www.aleyaharris. com/spark to get feedback from your peers and learn in a community setting.

CHAPTER 28

Write Your Radical Spark Signature Talk™ Topic Overview

**"Don't ever diminish the power of words.
Words move hearts and hearts move limbs."**
—Hamza Yusuf

Now, it's time to create your speaking pitch and topic. Here is where your brand and niche come into play. Your speaking topic must resonate with your intended audience while showcasing your unique value proposition. Remember, your talk overview isn't just for the event planners but also for the attendees deciding if your session is worth their time. They will use your overview to choose between you and other concurrent sessions. You need to make your session pop to get butts in seats in your room.

When you submit your topic for a speaking opportunity, often it's one of the only things people use to decide if they want you to speak. This means your overview needs to be compelling and clear from the get-go. Let's break down how to craft this essential component.

Start with the Problem

Begin with the problem you're solving. This should come straight from your Spark Storytelling Framework™ and Controlling Idea. Be specific and direct. Instead of being vague or overly poetic, outline the core issue that your talk addresses. This sets the stage for everything that follows.

For this section, I am going to use my Vanquish the Villains on Your Hero's Journey Radical Spark Signature Talk™ as an example. At the beginning of the speaking pitch I say, "You are the hero in your business's narrative, even though it may not feel like it when your energy is low and you're approaching burnout. It's hard to feel like the triumphant leader who has it all together."

That articulates the problem of burnout and touches upon how they feel, the true motivator of change.

Outline What Will Be Covered

Next, clearly articulate what your session will cover. Avoid flowery language and surprises. Attendees and event organizers want to know exactly what to expect.

For instance, "In this session, Aleya Harris steps into the role of your guide to walk you through the stages of the hero's journey and the common pitfalls present at each stage. She'll reveal her tried-and-true strategies for overcoming the villains in one's journey to keep positive energy flowing so you can rise out of burnout and discover freedom and abundance."

Not Attending Your Session Has a Price

Highlight the stakes by outlining the consequences of attending or not attending your session. What happens if they miss out? What benefits will they gain?

For example: "The stakes are clear—by attending, you'll learn to rise out of burnout and discover freedom and abundance. If you don't come to the session and get this positive energy, you're going to keep waking up knowing you will not reach your potential."

Articulate Three Tangible Takeaways

Almost every speaking overview submission asks for three key takeaways. These should be actionable and specific, and attendees should leave with concrete steps they can implement immediately.

For instance:

1. The three stages of the hero's journey and how they apply to business principles
2. Key techniques for getting unstuck in your business
3. How to map out a successful hero's journey for your business and personal life

Use buzzwords that are appealing to event planners and marketers like "actionable," "engaging," "immersive," "tangible," and "immediately implement." Corporate event planners and conference organizers do not want a session that is boring or one where someone just gets on stage to stroke their ego. They want a session that will make attendees come back and pay for their ticket next year. You should make it clear that you align and can deliver upon their goal of having a plethora of happy butts in seats.

Example Overview

Here's an example of a well-structured topic overview:

Vanquish the Villains

You are the hero in your business's narrative, even though it may not feel like it when your energy is low and you're approaching burnout. It's hard to feel like the triumphant leader that has it all together. But here's the secret—even the greatest heroes of all time need help. In this session, Aleya Harris steps into the role of your guide to walk you through the stages of the hero's journey and the common pitfalls present at each stage. She'll reveal her tried-and-true strategies for overcoming the villains in one's journey to keep positive energy flowing so you can rise out of burnout and discover freedom and abundance.

Three Tangible Takeaways:

1. The three stages of the hero's journey and how they apply to business principles
2. Key techniques for getting unstuck in your business
3. How to map out a successful hero's journey for your business and personal life

This example illustrates the problem, the content of the session, the stakes, and the actionable takeaways clearly and succinctly.

Checklist for Crafting Your Topic Overview

- Start with the Problem: Clearly define the problem your talk addresses.
- Outline What Will Be Covered: Specify the key points and content of your session.
- Success and Failure: Highlight the stakes of attending or missing your talk.
- Three Tangible Takeaways: Provide actionable and specific takeaways.
- Use Compelling Language: Include buzzwords like "actionable," "engaging," and "tangible."

Sample Templates

To help you start crafting your speaking topic overview, I've put together a few sample templates. These examples illustrate how to clearly define the problem, outline what your session will cover, and provide tangible takeaways. Use them as inspiration to create a compelling and engaging overview that resonates with your audience and sets you apart.

Template 1: Leadership in Crisis

Are you struggling to lead your team through turbulent times? In this session, Oreoluwa Adeoye will guide you through effective crisis leadership strategies. Discover how to maintain morale, take decisive actions, and steer your team to success even in the face of adversity. Don't miss your opportunity to be remembered as the leader who made a lasting impact on your organization during its time of need.

Three Tangible Takeaways:

1. Effective crisis management techniques
2. Strategies for maintaining team morale
3. Decision-making frameworks for turbulent times

Template 2: Wellness in the Workplace

Is your workplace suffering from low engagement and high stress? Join Jennifer Sanders to explore holistic wellness strategies that boost employee engagement and reduce stress. Learn practical approaches to creating a healthy work environment. High stress eventually leads to employee attrition and lower profits. Join us to prevent the people and money hemorrhaging before it starts.

Three Tangible Takeaways:

1. Holistic wellness strategies for the workplace
2. Techniques to reduce stress and increase engagement
3. Practical steps to implement wellness programs

Common Mistakes to Avoid

Before you dive into crafting your own speaking topic overview, it's important to be aware of some common pitfalls. Avoiding these mistakes will help you create a polished and professional presentation that captivates your audience and effectively communicates your message. Here are some common mistakes to watch out for as you develop your speaking topic overview.

1. Being Vague: Avoid ambiguous descriptions. Be clear and specific about what your session will cover.

2. Ignoring the Stakes: Make sure to outline the consequences of attending or not attending your session.

3. Overloading with Information: Focus on three key takeaways rather than overwhelming the audience with too much information.

4. Neglecting the Buzzwords: Use language that is attractive to event planners and attendees.

Your speaking overview is a crucial element of your pitch. It's your chance to capture the attention of event organizers and potential attendees. A compelling overview that clearly articulates the problem, outlines what will be covered, and provides tangible takeaways can set you apart from the crowd.

Once you've crafted your overview, you're almost ready to pitch. Remember, the more you speak, the more you'll get booked. It's a wonderful cycle where people begin to know you, refer you, and invite you to speak at more events.

Now, go forth and create your speaking overview.

Spark Steps

- Write your Radical Spark Signature Talk™ Topic Overview. Make sure to include the three key takeaways.
- At this point, I get that you have a lot to write and it may feel foreign to you, especially if you aren't a marketer. If you want my one-on-one help, head to www.aleyaharris.com/spark-box to schedule a marketing review call. I will help you make sense out of everything you need to do to be ready to get on stage.

CHAPTER 29

Finding & Getting the Gig

"If you build it, they will come" is not gonna work out well for you. You need to take inspired action to reach your speaking goals.

Now that you've nailed down your Radical Spark Signature Talk™ Outline and Topic Overview, it's time to book that talk.

Getting on stage as a speaker is not difficult. Let me repeat that for the people in the back: getting on stage to speak is not difficult. When you first start out, it feels like a herculean task, like, "Oh my gosh, are they gonna choose me?" But the truth is, getting on stage is easier than you might think. There are venues everywhere, and there are thousands of event organizers out there, hungry for speakers. The key is to start speaking and keep speaking—speaking begets more speaking opportunities.

Let's talk about some of the most surefire routes to the stage.

Calls for Speakers

Calls for speakers are announcements from events, associations, and conferences seeking presenters. They say, "Hey, we're looking for speakers for our upcoming event. Submit your proposal here."

The easiest first step is to Google "call for speakers" and see what pops up. You can also type in "call for speakers" along with your preferred locations or industries, like "2026 calls for speakers Los Angeles" or "call for speakers engineering." Most likely, there are pages and pages of people looking for someone just like you to grace their audience with your knowledge and energy. Our goal is to help you complete the call for speakers form in a way that increases your chances of being chosen.

Submitting to calls for speakers is an essential part of growing your speaking career. Events are often looking for fresh, engaging voices to present valuable content, and a well-crafted submission can set you apart from the crowd.

Submit your proposals, keep track of your submissions, and don't get discouraged by delays—there's often a gap between submission and acceptance.

One strategy I used was to set a daily goal to submit at least one call for speakers. I kept track with two shot glasses and five straws, moving one straw each day from an empty glass to a sparkly, decorative one when I submitted a proposal. This visual and physical act kept me motivated and consistent. Remember, consistency is key to getting booked. You can't become a professional speaker without putting yourself out into the world.

Here are some best practices for effectively submitting to calls for speakers and increasing your chances of being selected.

1. Understand the Event
   Before submitting your application, thoroughly research the event. Understand its theme, the type of audience it attracts, and its overall mission. Review previous events to see the types of speakers and topics that have been successful. Tailoring your submission to align with the event's goals and audience can significantly enhance your chances of being selected.

2. Follow the Guidelines
   Each call for speakers will have specific guidelines and requirements. These may include word counts, formats, deadlines, and specific information about your talk. Adhering to these guidelines is crucial. Missing a deadline or failing to follow instructions can result in your submission being disqualified, no matter how great your content is.

3. Use Your Radical Spark Signature Talk ™ Overview
   Your talk's overview is often the first thing reviewers will see, so make it compelling, like I taught you. Clearly state the topic of your talk, the problem it addresses, and the key takeaways for the audience. Use clear, concise language and avoid jargon. The goal is to make your talk sound engaging and valuable at a glance.

4. Highlight Your Unique Perspective
   What makes your talk different from others on the same topic? Highlight your unique perspective, experiences, or approach. If you have a special method, case study, or personal story that adds depth to your talk, make sure to mention it. Your UVP should shine through your abstract and title.

5. Include a Strong Bio
   Your speaker bio is an opportunity to showcase your expertise and experience. Include relevant credentials, past speaking engagements, and any unique qualifications you have. Make sure your bio reflects your personality and aligns with your brand.

6. Provide Supporting Materials
   If the submission process allows, include links to videos of your past talks, your speaker one sheet, and testimonials from previous engagements. These materials provide evidence of your speaking skills and help event organizers see you in action. Ensure your video clips showcase you at your best.

7. Be Clear About Your AV Needs
   If your presentation requires specific audiovisual equipment or setup, mention it in your application. This helps event organizers plan and ensures you have what you need to deliver a great talk. Being upfront about your needs can prevent issues on the day of your presentation.

8. Proofread Your Submission
   Before hitting submit, carefully proofread your application. Errors or typos can make a bad impression and suggest a lack of attention to detail. Consider having a colleague or friend review your submission for any mistakes or areas that could be improved.

9. Follow Up Politely
   After submitting your application, note the timeline for decisions, if provided. If you haven't heard back within the expected timeframe, a polite follow-up email is appropriate.

Thank them for considering your application and express your continued interest in participating in their event.

10. Keep a Record of Your Submissions
    Maintain a spreadsheet or document tracking the events you've applied to, including submission dates, deadlines, and follow-up notes. This helps you stay organized and ensures you don't miss any important deadlines or opportunities to follow up.

Submitting to calls for speakers is a strategic process that requires careful planning and attention to detail. By understanding the event, crafting a compelling abstract, highlighting your unique perspective, and providing strong supporting materials, you can increase your chances of being selected. Remember to follow up politely and keep track of your submissions to stay organized. With these best practices, you'll be well on your way to securing speaking engagements that elevate your profile and expand your reach.

Direct Cold Pitching

Submitting calls for speakers will get you on stages if you constantly submit a quality talk. However, it can be difficult to find paid opportunities through calls for speakers. If you would like to be more targeted in your approach to unearthing opportunities where the event organizers shell out cold, hard cash, you will want to learn how to pitch yourself directly.

A cold pitch is a direct outreach to potential clients, showcasing your value and proposing your talk. Think of it as your elevator pitch but more detailed and tailored to the needs of the event planners you're reaching out to.

Here's the format I recommend and use myself:

1. Problem Your Talk Solves: Start with the issue your talk addresses.

2. Your One Liner: Introduce yourself succinctly.

3. Signature Talk Title: Present the name of your talk.

4. Plan: Outline what the event planner can expect.

5. Call to Action: Clearly state the next steps.

6. Success/Failure: Highlight the stakes and the potential outcomes of booking you.

Example Pitch Breakdown

Let's walk through an example of what a cold pitch might look like:

Email Subject: Transform Your Event with Engaging and Insightful Storytelling

Hi [Event Planner's Name],

Are any of your current clients looking for a keynote presenter or workshop leader to help them solve issues with toxic workplace cultures, low engagement, or communication breakdowns? If so, I can help.

My name is Aleya Harris, and I am a Strategic Storytelling Consultant and award-winning speaker. I help business leaders overcome communication and differentiation challenges by sharing radically authentic stories that transform workplace culture and carve unique market niches.

My signature talk is "Crafting Cultural Change: The Transformative Power of Radically Authentic Storytelling." To secure me to edutain your audience, the next step is to schedule a call to discuss your event.

Once you pick your topic and sign your contract, I will show up and make you look amazing to your client by delivering an engaging session with tangible takeaways.

Booking me as your next speaker will elevate your event experience and prevent you from the disappointment of a lackluster session that drags down the vibe you so meticulously crafted.

Are you available for a quick call on Tuesday at 10:00 a.m.?

I know I can help you get rave reviews, and I'm excited to chat soon.

Best,

Aleya

P.S. I've attached my speaker one sheet so you can learn more about me and my topic. Also, click [here] for a link to my media kit.

P.P.S. Don't have an immediate need? No problem. I would still love to chat to get acquainted and get a better understanding of the types of speakers you typically book for your clients.

Tips for Crafting Your Pitch

- Tailor Each Pitch: Customize your pitch for each specific event planner. Don't use a one-size-fits-all approach.
- Keep It Focused: Pitch only one talk at a time. Choose the one that best matches the audience and aligns with what you are currently selling.
- Be Clear and Direct: Your pitch should be straightforward and easy to follow. Avoid jargon and keep your language professional but approachable.
- Include Supporting Materials: Attach your speaker one sheet and provide a link to your media kit for more information.

- Be OK with Being On Hold: Often, corporate event planners and organizers don't know if they will need you and may feel odd responding if there isn't an immediate fit. Feel free to assure them that you are OK with being added to their list of potential speakers. You will check in periodically to see if there is a match and to keep them updated on any new topics.

During a cold pitch email, you are selling yourself as a transformational thought leader. Just like any sales process, follow-up is key. You can't expect to send one direct email and get booked every time. I encourage you to be persistent and keep good records of who you contacted and when. If you are able, the follow up is a great thing to outsource to an assistant. Regardless, stay positive in the process. You attract what you think about most, so focus your thoughts on ideas of connecting with people who will eagerly book you.

Use this checklist to ensure you've covered all the essential elements of a successful cold pitch:

1. Research the Event and Audience: Understand the event's theme, audience, and past speakers.

2. Personalize Your Email: Use the event planner's name and reference specifics about the event or their organization.

3. State the Problem: Clearly articulate the problem your talk solves.

4. Introduce Yourself: Include your one liner to succinctly introduce yourself.

5. Present Your Talk: State the title of your signature talk.

6. Outline the Plan: Explain the steps the event planner needs to take to book you.

7. Include a Call to Action: Provide a clear next step, such as scheduling a call.

8. Highlight the Stakes: Emphasize the benefits of booking you and the potential downsides of not doing so.

9. Attach Supporting Materials: Include your speaker one sheet and a link to your media kit.

10. Proofread: Double-check your pitch for any errors or typos.

11. Send: Send your email and track responses. Schedule follow-ups if needed.

Crafting a compelling cold pitch is a crucial step in getting booked as a speaker. By following the steps outlined in this section and using the provided checklist, you'll be well on your way to creating pitches that capture attention and open doors to exciting speaking opportunities. Remember, persistence and personalization are key. Good luck, and happy pitching!

Speaker Agents and Bureaus

A speaker agent can be a valuable asset. You pay a speaker agent to actively seek paid speaking gigs for you, using their network and expertise. If you can afford it, having an agent can save you time and increase your booking frequency. You could also employ and train a virtual assistant (VA) to help you seek, apply, and book gigs if you have the time to manage the process.

Speaker bureaus work similarly to agents but often represent multiple speakers and get paid by the clients booking you. While bureaus can help you land bigger gigs, they might not always have your best financial interests at heart since they are paid by the event organizers. They have to walk the line between getting their client the best price, getting you a good rate, and getting a commission for themselves based on your final speaker fee. Also, you may need to get some speaking under your belt first before you are a good candidate for a bureau. Most speaker bureaus put effort behind speakers with big names, very visible backgrounds, or authors. You can be on their roster without checking those boxes, but you may not get the same attention. Check out speakers bureaus, but you should also explore other methods to get on stage.

Networking with Similar Speakers

Look at testimonials of speakers you admire or those slightly ahead of you. The people who wrote those testimonials are often the ones who book speakers. Reach out to them with your information, highlighting how your style is similar yet unique. Networking with fellow speakers can also lead to referrals and recommendations, helping you get booked more often.

Corporate Event Planners

Corporate event planners are often the decision-makers for booking speakers at larger events. Networking with them through organizations like Meeting Planners International (MPI) can open doors to significant opportunities. Submitting to speak at MPI events can also increase your visibility.

Destination Management Organizations and Companies

Organizations like Visit Los Angeles or Visit Las Vegas often have connections with speakers and can be great resources for getting booked. Networking with these organizations can lead to speaking opportunities.

Associations

Associations are fantastic for finding speaking gigs. They frequently hold events, conferences, and have annual calls for speakers. If you know your niche, search for all related associations and submit to speak at their events. This can help you get on stage and gain valuable experience. Look for association events where the audience is comprised of key decision-makers.

LinkedIn and Social Media

LinkedIn is a treasure trove for finding speaking gigs. Use it to connect with speaker bureaus, associations, corporate event planners, and other relevant contacts. Investing in LinkedIn Premium and Sales Navigator can provide you with even more tools to find the right people. Tools like Meet Alfred can help automate and personalize your outreach, inviting potential clients to podcasts, workshops, or other engaging offers. This approach builds your thought leadership and creates a pipeline of opportunities.

Remember, the Internet is a fantastic resource. Start with calls for speakers, then move to direct outreach and the other methods. Focus on places and events that excite you, and soon enough, you'll find yourself on stage, sharing your message with the world.

Spark Steps

- Research at least 10 calls for speakers and set a deadline to submit to them within the next two weeks.
- Research at least 10 companies you would like to pitch to directly within the next two weeks.
- Create your pitch email.
- Locate the email addresses of your desired companies and make your pitch.
- Accountability is hard, but it is much more manageable when done in a community. Head to www.aleyaharris.com/spark to join Spark the Stage™ and find an accountability buddy. Together, you can ensure that you hit your pitching goals and see your names in lights.

CHAPTER 30

Create Your Media Kit

"Eighty percent of success is showing up."
—Woody Allen

When you're pitching, whether through cold pitches or submitting calls for speakers, you need to make it easy for people to get all of your information at once in a downloadable way. That's where a media kit comes in. A media kit should include your headshot, your bio, your reels (videos of you speaking), your one-pager, and your testimonials. If you're just beginning, you might not have all of these things at once. That's OK. Add in what you have and adjust as you go.

I love to put my media kit in a Google Drive folder where I can swap things out whenever necessary. I have a URL that never changes (www.aleyaharris.com/media-kit), but what's in the folder gets adjusted and updated as I add new materials, have new photo shoots, update my topics, or tweak my bio.

Your media kit is incredibly important. In fact, I'd recommend doing this before you even build out your website. A media kit is actionable. You can send it to people, they can get a feel for who you are and what you're doing right away, and they can use this information to book you.

Components of a Media Kit

1. Headshot:
   Your headshot is the first impression you give. Ensure it's professional and reflects your brand. If you don't have a professional headshot yet, use a well-lit photo taken with a good-quality camera.

2. Bio:
   Your bio should be concise but impactful, giving a snapshot of who you are and why you're the perfect speaker. Check out the section below for detailed instructions on how to write a good, radically authentic speaker bio.

3. Reels:
   You need to have videos of you speaking. This is imperative for people to understand your style as a speaker. If you've never spoken on a stage before, start with at least having a video of you speaking directly to the camera. Sit down in front of your computer and just talk about your speaking topics or recite your Radical Spark Signature Talk ™ Overview. Set up a camera and record yourself standing and delivering the presentation in your office or rent out a conference room.

As you start getting out there on people's stages, request that they include video as part of your compensation. If you are taking responsibility for your own video recording, don't feel obligated to spend thousands of dollars on your video creation when you are first starting out. You can use a cell phone and tripod to capture your stage performance. You just need something event organizers can see to determine your style and capability. Video is incredibly important in the speaking world.

There are two main types of reels:

- Straight-Up Speaking: These show you directly speaking to an audience, allowing event organizers to see your style. You should have five-minute clips that showcase you at your best.
- Sizzle Reels: These are more like movie trailers with higher production value and showcase your speaking engagements' highlights.

Both types of reels are valuable. A speaker's bureau might prefer sizzle reels for a polished presentation, while event organizers might want straightforward speaking reels to assess your delivery.

4. One-Pager:
   Your one-pager is a condensed version of your media kit, typically designed to be a quick overview. It includes your headshot, a brief bio, authority logos, Radical Spark Signature Talk™ overview, key takeaways, and a call to action to book you. It can also include additional topics, testimonials, and more photos.

   I created mine in Canva in less than an hour. Keep it clean, professional, and polished. Use a template if you need to, but ensure it reflects your brand. You can see an example of my one-pager in my media kit at www.aleyaharris.com/media-kit.

5. Testimonials:
   Include testimonials from your speaking engagements. If you don't have those yet, use testimonials from your work or clients that highlight your skills and character. These testimonials will translate your value on stage.

   Remember, this is an iterative process. Your media kit will grow and evolve as you do. Don't let perfection keep you from getting started. Having nothing will definitely not help you get on stage.

Writing a Radically Authentic Speaker Bio

Writing my own bio was the bane of my existence. It always sounded wrong. When I asked someone else to write it, it didn't sound right either. I was so wrapped up in trying to capture every facet of my life in a few paragraphs that I was hard to please. However, once I got strategic with how I structured my bio, and really thought about its *purpose*, I was thrilled because I knew that it was formatted to help me get booked more often. I am going to take a deep dive into bio writing so you don't have to struggle like I did.

Your speaker bio is more than just a list of accomplishments—it's your chance to make a memorable first impression and showcase your unique personality and expertise. A radically authentic speaker bio highlights your qualifications and gives potential clients and audiences a sense of who you are and what makes you unique. Here's how to craft a compelling, authentic speaker bio that stands out.

1. Start with a Strong Opening
    Your opening sentence should grab the reader's attention and give them a quick sense of who you are. It could be a powerful statement, a surprising fact, or a concise summary of your expertise. For example:

    "Aleya Harris is a dynamic storyteller and marketing maven who transforms organizations through the power of Radically Authentic Strategic Storytelling™."

2. Highlight Your Unique Value Proposition (UVP)
    Include your UVP early in your bio. Your UVP is the unique solution you offer and the promise of value your audience can expect. Make sure it aligns with your overall brand and messaging:

    "Aleya's unique approach combines her extensive experience in marketing with her passion for storytelling to help businesses and individuals unlock their full potential and achieve lasting impact."

3. Showcase Your Credentials
    Include your most relevant and impressive credentials, but do it in a way that tells a story. Instead of simply listing your degrees or awards, weave them into a narrative that illustrates your journey and expertise:

    "With a background as a professional chef and a marketer, Aleya has traveled the world, working with celebrity clients and building a successful strategic storytelling consultancy. She is also a strategic storytelling consultant, helping leaders craft compelling narratives that resonate."

4. Include Personal Touches
    Share a bit about your personality, interests, and values. These details help humanize you and make your bio more relatable and engaging. Be authentic and let your true self shine through:

    "When she's not on stage or strategizing with clients, Aleya can be found practicing hot yoga, experimenting with new recipes, or exploring nature with her toddler, Ruby Coral."

5. Highlight Your Speaking Experience
    Detail your speaking experience and any notable engagements.
    Showing how you've been successful builds credibility and
    shows that you are a seasoned speaker. Mention specific events,
    audiences, and the impact of your talks:

    "Aleya is an award-winning international speaker who has
    captivated audiences at conferences, workshops, and corporate
    events. Her engaging and transformative presentations have
    inspired countless leaders to embrace their authentic selves
    and create meaningful change."

6. End with a Call to Action
    Conclude your bio with a call to action that invites event
    organizers to book you or audiences to connect with you.
    Make it clear how they can reach you and what steps they
    should take:

    "Ready to transform your event with radically authentic
    storytelling? Book Aleya Harris today and discover the power
    of a speaker who connects. Visit www.aleyaharris.com to learn
    more and get in touch."

Example Bio

Here's a sample speaker bio that incorporates all these elements:

*Aleya Harris is a dynamic storyteller and marketing maven who
transforms organizations through the power of Radically Authentic
Strategic Storytelling™. Aleya's unique approach combines her extensive
experience in marketing with her passion for storytelling to help
businesses and individuals unlock their full potential and achieve
lasting impact.*

*With a background as a professional chef and a marketer, Aleya
has traveled the world, working with celebrity clients and building*

a successful strategic storytelling consultancy. She is also a strategic storytelling consultant, helping leaders craft compelling narratives that resonate. When she's not on stage or strategizing with clients, Aleya can be found practicing hot yoga, experimenting with new recipes, or playing in the park with her toddler, Ruby Coral.

Aleya is an award-winning international speaker who has captivated audiences at conferences, workshops, and corporate events. Her engaging and transformative presentations have inspired countless leaders to embrace their authentic selves and create meaningful change.

Ready to transform your event with radically authentic storytelling? Book Aleya Harris today and discover the power of a speaker who truly connects. Visit www.aleyaharris.com to learn more and get in touch.

Fill-in-the-Blank Speaker Bio

Crafting a compelling speaker bio can be daunting, but having a structured framework can make the process much easier and boost your confidence. Use the fill-in-the-blank format below to create a bio highlighting your strengths, personal touch, and call to action. It will ensure that your bio is engaging and helps you book gigs.

[Your Name] is a [descriptor – e.g., passionate, dynamic, insightful] [your profession] who specializes in [your niche or area of expertise]. [Your Name]'s unique approach combines [describe your unique approach or methodology] with a deep understanding of [relevant field/industry]. With a background in [your background/education], [Your Name] has [mention notable achievements or experiences].

As a [your profession], [Your Name] has successfully [mention specific accomplishments or impact]. Their work has helped [mention types of clients or industries you've worked with] achieve [mention results or benefits].

[Your Name] is not just a [your profession]; they are a [descriptor – e.g., dedicated, committed] partner in their clients' success. [Personal

touch – e.g., when not working with clients, they enjoy (hobbies/ interests) and (personal activities)].

[Your Name] is a sought-after speaker who has delivered [mention types of presentations – e.g., impactful presentations, engaging workshops] at [mention types of events – e.g., industry conferences, executive retreats]. Their [descriptor – e.g., engaging, insightful] talks have inspired audiences to [mention the main takeaway or impact of your talks].

Ready to [mention what you help your audience achieve]? Book [Your Name] today and discover the power of [mention your unique approach or methodology]. Visit [your website] to learn more and get in touch.

Here is another example from my fictitious friend, Jimmy Chen, using that framework:

Jimmy Chen is a results-driven business consultant and EOS (Entrepreneurial Operating System) expert who empowers companies to achieve their highest potential through strategic planning and execution. Jimmy's unique approach combines his deep understanding of business operations with his passion for helping leaders and teams align and thrive.

With a background in management consulting and years of hands-on experience in the corporate world, Jimmy has successfully guided numerous organizations through the complexities of EOS implementation. He has a proven track record of transforming businesses, enhancing operational efficiency, and driving sustainable growth.

Jimmy is not just a consultant; he is a dedicated partner in his clients' success. His commitment to excellence and personalized approach have earned him a reputation as a trusted advisor who delivers tangible results. When he's not working with clients, Jimmy enjoys hiking in the mountains, experimenting with new cooking recipes, and volunteering at local non-profits.

Jimmy is a sought-after speaker who has delivered impactful presentations at industry conferences, workshops, and executive retreats. His engaging and insightful talks have inspired business leaders to embrace EOS and transform their organizations from the inside out.

Ready to take your business to the next level with expert EOS implementation? Book Jimmy Chen today and discover the power of a consultant who truly understands and cares about your success. Visit www.jimmychenconsulting.com to learn more and get in touch.

Short Bio Template

Event organizers often ask for a short version of your bio to introduce you before you come on stage. Here is a short bio template and example.

Introducing [Your Name], a [descriptor – e.g., passionate, dynamic, insightful] [your profession] specializing in [your niche or area of expertise]. With a unique approach that combines [describe your unique approach or methodology] and a deep understanding of [relevant field/industry], [Your Name] has helped [mention types of clients or industries you've worked with] achieve [mention results or benefits]. Today, [Your Name] is here to share their insights on [mention topic]. Please join me in welcoming [Your Name].

Let's look at how this would read for our same fictitious friend, Jimmy Chen.

Introducing Jimmy Chen, a dynamic business consultant specializing in EOS implementation. With a unique approach that combines strategic planning and a deep understanding of business operations, Jimmy has helped numerous organizations achieve remarkable growth. Today, Jimmy is here to share his insights on transforming business operations through EOS. Please join me in welcoming Jimmy Chen.

Writing a radically authentic speaker bio is about more than listing your accomplishments; it's about sharing your story in a way that resonates with your audience. By starting with a strong opening, highlighting your UVP, showcasing your credentials, including personal touches, detailing your speaking experience, and ending with a call to action, you can craft a bio that stands out and attracts the right opportunities. Let your authenticity shine through and create a bio that not only informs but also inspires.

Spark Steps

Assemble Your Media Kit:

- Headshot: Get a professional or well-lit, high-quality photo that represents your brand.
- Bio: Write a concise and compelling bio that showcases your unique value proposition and background.
- Reels: Record yourself delivering key parts of your presentation. Use both straight-up speaking and sizzle reels.
- One-Pager: Design a one-pager in Canva or another tool. Include your headshot, brief bio, authority logos, signature talk overview, key takeaways, and call to action.
- Testimonials: Gather testimonials from past speaking engagements or from clients and colleagues that highlight your skills and character.

Organize Your Media Kit:
- Create a Google Drive folder or a similar online repository for your media kit.
- Ensure all elements are up-to-date and accessible via a permanent URL.

Request Video Footage:
- Whenever you speak, ask event organizers if they can provide a video recording.
- If they can't, bring your own equipment or have a friend record your presentation.

Iterate and Update:
- Continuously update your media kit with new videos, photos, testimonials, and any changes to your bio or speaking topics.

Create Your Speaker Bio:
- Use the provided fill-in-the-blank template to draft a compelling speaker bio.
- Ensure your bio aligns with your brand and highlights your unique value proposition.

Develop a Short Bio for Introductions:
- Craft a brief version of your bio to use for stage introductions.

Review and Polish:
- Ensure all media kit and bio elements are polished, professional, and aligned with your brand.
- Seek feedback from trusted colleagues or mentors to refine your materials.

Distribute Your Media Kit:

- Share your media kit with event organizers, upload it to your website, and include it in your pitches.
- Use it to book speaking engagements and showcase your professionalism and preparedness.

Want to get feedback on your media kit? I would be happy to take a look. Head to the Spark Box at www.aleyaharris.com/spark-box to schedule a marketing review call.

You could also join Spark the Stage™ to share your media kit with the community to get feedback. You'll also get to see examples of theirs to get new ideas on how to make yours even better. Sign up for Spark the Stage™ at www.aleyaharris.com/spark.

CHAPTER 31

Market Yourself as a Speaker

**"Too many people overvalue what they are
not and undervalue what they are."**
—Malcolm Forbes

Although you want to be proactive and go after your speaking gigs, you also want to start building a presence for yourself online and creating content that supports your message to create a more robust thought leadership platform. That's where marketing comes in. For me, marketing is the art and science of building lucrative relationships. The whole purpose of any marketing activity is to create a relationship with someone who will buy from you later or connect you with someone who will buy from you.

There are several things you can do, but these are the four things I suggest getting set up for yourself as a speaker:

Create a Website Landing Page

Your website landing page is where people can find all the information they need about you as a speaker. You should create your landing page after you've put together your media kit. Your landing page can be your entire website if it's just one page dedicated to your speaking, or it can be a stand-alone page on your current site. For example, my speaking page is www.aleyaharris.com/speaking. The rest of my website goes more in-depth about me, my podcast, my businesses, and other details. But when someone is specifically looking for a speaker, they can go directly to that page.

Your website should cover the problem you solve, and the clear wins you achieve. It should include your reels, testimonials, speaking topics, and, most importantly, how people can book you. There should be a clear "Schedule a Call" button, a form, or contact information that makes it easy for people to contact you.

Here's a checklist to ensure you include all the necessary elements and follow best practices:

Essential Elements

1. Clear Header with Your Name and Title: Ensure your name and title (e.g., Keynote Speaker, Motivational Speaker, etc.) are prominently displayed at the top of the page.

2. Professional Bio: Include a well-crafted bio that highlights your expertise, experience, and unique value proposition.

3. High-Quality Photos: Use professional photos of yourself, including headshots and images of you speaking at events.

4. Speaking Topics: List your main speaking topics with brief descriptions for each. Make it clear what you specialize in.

5. Reels and Videos: Embed high-quality videos of your past speaking engagements to showcase your skills and style.

6. Testimonials: Include quotes and testimonials from past clients or audience members to build credibility.

7. Clear Call-to-Action (CTA): Provide an easy way for visitors to book you, such as a "Schedule a Call" button, a contact form, or your email address.

8. Contact Information: Ensure your contact information is easily accessible, including email address, phone number, and links to your social media profiles.

9. Downloadable Media Kit: Include a link to download your media kit, which should contain your bio, headshots, reels, speaking topics, testimonials, and contact information.

Best Practices

- Consistent Branding: Ensure your website's design, colors, fonts, and images reflect your personal brand consistently.
- Mobile-Friendly Design: Make sure your website is responsive and looks great on all devices, including smartphones and tablets.
- Fast Loading Speed: Optimize images and content to ensure your website loads quickly to prevent visitors from leaving.
- Easy Navigation: Use a simple and intuitive menu to help visitors find the information they need quickly.
- Engaging and Concise Copy: Write engaging, concise, and clear copy that captures your personality and effectively communicates your message.
- SEO Optimization: Use relevant keywords, meta tags, and alt text for images to improve your search engine ranking and make it easier for potential clients to find you.

- Regular Updates: Keep your website content fresh by regularly updating it with new speaking topics, testimonials, videos, and blog posts, if applicable.
- Analytics Tracking: Set up Google Analytics or another analytics tool to track visitor behavior and measure your website's effectiveness.

When developing your speaker page, getting caught up in the details or getting all in your feelings about colors and fonts is easy. My friend, I am here to remind you to keep your eyes on the prize. If you remember nothing else, keep the following tips in mind when you are building your speaker page:

- Make It Easy to Book You: Your primary goal is to get booked for speaking engagements, so make it effortless for event organizers to contact you. Include a prominent "Book Now" or "Schedule a Call" button repeated several times on your landing page.
- Showcase Your Expertise: Use your bio, videos, and testimonials to highlight your expertise and establish yourself as an authority in your field. The more you demonstrate your skills and experience, the more appealing you will be to potential clients.
- Use High-Quality Visuals: Invest in professional photos and videos to give your landing page a polished, professional look. High-quality visuals can significantly affect how you are perceived.
- Be Authentic: Your landing page should reflect your unique personality and style. Be genuine in your messaging and design to attract clients who resonate with your brand.
- Optimize for Search Engines: Ensure your landing page is SEO-friendly by using relevant keywords and phrases that

your potential clients might be searching for. Keywords are one of the major ways to help you rank higher in search results and attract more visitors. Remember that you can also employ a more robust SEO strategy.

Right about now, I know you are super tempted to go out and find a bunch of other speakers' websites and stitch all the parts you like to create a Frankenstein's monster site to call your very own. You're doing that already, aren't you? Gotcha.

Give your Google finger a rest for a second and instead start to envision what you want your radically authentic site to look like based on what you know about your talk, your goals, and your purpose. What is the feeling you want to leave with a corporate event planner or association client who visits? What final result would make you feel proud?

Always start with you and the guidance of your Radically Authentic Self before you hop onto the internet and become a carbon copy of someone else. That minimizes all of the work you've done up until now. Remember, you already know the answers. Just allow them to come forward.

Use LinkedIn and Social Media Strategically

Most event organizers are on LinkedIn. I encourage you to post regularly on LinkedIn, at least a couple of times a week, about things related to your Radical Spark Signature Talk™ and your business. Talk about why you speak about what you do, and develop a content strategy that expands upon your expertise. Make sure you don't try to be everywhere. Pick one or two platforms and stick with them.

I chose LinkedIn and Instagram as my primary social media platforms. LinkedIn is where most of my clients hang out for speaking and consulting services, while Instagram is where budding speakers who want a more personal insight into my life follow me. Ensure you choose platforms that make sense for you. Also, video is not just the future; it's the now. Create videos and post them on social media of you speaking and sharing ideas. Videos are a great way to promote yourself.

Let me give you an example of how to do this well using another fictional friend, Keisha Jones. Keisha Jones is an ancestral spiritual healer who focuses on African pre-colonial traditions. She speaks about mindfulness and well-being in corporate environments. Her Radical Spark Signature Talk ™ is "Mindfulness and Wellbeing: Embracing Ancestral Wisdom in Modern Corporate Environments."

Below is her sample content calendar for two weeks with short description snippets showcasing how she can effectively use LinkedIn to share her message and connect with her audience.

Sample LinkedIn Content Calendar for Keisha Jones

Monday: Video Post
- Topic: Introduction to Ancestral Wisdom
- Description: "Grand rising, LinkedIn family! Today, I want to introduce you to ancestral wisdom and its importance in our modern lives. Learn how reconnecting with traditional African religions can enhance mindfulness and well-being in the workplace. Watch the video to find out more!"
- Format: Video (2-3 minutes)

Wednesday: LinkedIn Newsletter
- Topic: The Benefits of Mindfulness in Corporate Settings
- Description: "In this week's newsletter, I delve into the numerous benefits of mindfulness practices within corporate environments. Discover how integrating these practices

can increase productivity, reduce stress, and create a more harmonious workplace. Subscribe to stay updated on tips and insights!"

- Format: LinkedIn Newsletter

Thursday: Text Post with Image

- Topic: A Client's Success Story
- Description: "I'm excited to share a success story from one of my recent corporate workshops. By incorporating ancestral mindfulness practices, this team significantly improved their overall wellbeing and collaboration."
- Format: Client testimonial image

Monday: Poll

- Topic: Favorite Mindfulness Practices
- Description: "I'm curious to know, what are your favorite mindfulness practices? Share your thoughts below! #Mindfulness #Wellbeing #CorporateCulture"
- Options: Guided Meditation, Journaling, Breathing Exercises, Ancestral Practices
- Format: LinkedIn Poll

Tuesday: Article Share

- Topic: Recent Research on Mindfulness and Productivity
- Description: "I've been reading up on recent research about mindfulness's impact on workplace productivity. This article from [source] offers fascinating insights that align with the principles of ancestral wisdom. Check it out and let me know your thoughts! #Research #Mindfulness #Productivity"
- Format: Shared article with a personal commentary

Wednesday: LinkedIn Live

- Topic: Q&A Session on Ancestral Spiritual Healing
- Description: "Join me for a live Q&A session where I'll be answering your questions about ancestral spiritual healing and how you can apply it in corporate settings. Don't miss this opportunity to learn and engage! #LinkedInLive #Mindfulness #Wellbeing"
- Format: LinkedIn Live Video

Friday: Inspirational Quote

- Topic: Reflecting on the Week
- Description: "As we wrap up the week, I leave you with an inspiring quote from an African proverb: 'Wisdom is like a baobab tree; no one individual can embrace it.' Let's continue to embrace collective wisdom and mindfulness."
- Format: Text post with an image of a baobab tree

By following a content calendar like this, Keisha Jones can maintain a consistent and engaging presence on LinkedIn. She can build her brand, share her expertise, and connect with potential clients and speaking opportunities.

Develop a Content Strategy

Don't post willy-nilly. You need a content strategy. What is the Controlling Idea. of your content? (Hint: It could be the same as the one you used for your Radical Spark Signature Talk™.) What is the Controlling Idea of your social media presence and your brand? How can you break that down into three to five main subject areas or content pillars and only talk about those things?

What you talk about is what you become known for. I talk about Radically Authentic Strategic Storytelling™ and speaking.

That's it. Guess what? I'm known for Radically Authentic Strategic Storytelling™ and speaking. Focus on things that make you money, bring you joy, and serve others.

Below are some questions to get you started with creating your professional speaker content strategy.

Content Strategy Builder

1. Identify Your Goals
   - What do you want to achieve with your content? (e.g., increase visibility, book more speaking gigs, grow your audience)
2. Define Your Audience
   - Who are you creating content for? (e.g., corporate leaders, entrepreneurs, wellness enthusiasts)
   - What are their pain points and interests?
3. Choose Your Platforms
   - Where will you share your content? (e.g., LinkedIn, Instagram, YouTube)
4. Content Themes
   - What topics will you cover? (e.g., leadership, mindfulness, innovation)
   - How do these topics relate to your speaking engagements?
5. Content Types
   - What formats will you use? (e.g., articles, videos, polls, live sessions)
6. Content Calendar
   - Plan your content schedule (e.g., daily, weekly)
   - Ensure a mix of content types and themes
7. Engagement and Interaction
   - How will you interact with your audience? (e.g., responding to comments, hosting Q&A sessions)

8. Measure and Adjust
   - How will you measure success? (e.g., engagement rates, new speaking inquiries)
   - Regularly review and adjust your strategy based on performance

Example Content Strategy for Keisha Jones

Let's see how our fictitious friend from before, Keisha Jones, might create her content strategy.

1. Identify Your Goals
   - Increase visibility as a thought leader in mindfulness and wellbeing
   - Book more speaking engagements in corporate environments
2. Define Your Audience
   - Corporate leaders and HR professionals interested in enhancing workplace wellbeing
   - Employees looking for ways to reduce stress and improve productivity
3. Choose Your Platforms
   - LinkedIn, Instagram, YouTube
4. Content Themes
   - Mindfulness practices in the workplace
   - Benefits of ancestral spiritual healing
   - Strategies for stress reduction and productivity
5. Content Types
   - Articles, short videos, live sessions, polls, quotes, client testimonials
6. Content Calendar
   - Monday: Video on mindfulness techniques (YouTube)
   - Tuesday: Article on the benefits of ancestral healing (LinkedIn)

- Wednesday: Client testimonial (Instagram)
- Monday: Poll on favorite mindfulness practices (LinkedIn)
- Tuesday: Live Q&A session (YouTube)
- Wednesday: Inspirational quote (Instagram)

7. Engagement and Interaction
   - Respond to comments on all platforms
   - Host monthly webinars and live Q&A sessions
8. Measure and Adjust
   - Track engagement rates on each platform
   - Monitor the number of speaking inquiries received
   - Adjust content themes and formats based on what resonates most with the audience.

By following this template and example, you can create a content strategy tailored to your goals and audience. Effectively market yourself as a speaker and achieve your objectives.

Leverage Public Relations (PR)

PR will always have a special place in my heart because it helped me build myself as a thought leader. By effectively using PR and speaking, I built my business to $250,000 in revenue in six months. PR involves using other people's platforms to get your message out and leveraging their audience to get yourself, your ideas, and your content in front of them. Tactics could be through blog posts on other people's platforms, podcasts, newsletters, news features, and even TV appearances.

Think about it this way: someone out there has already done the work to gather your ideal audience. So why work so hard to build it from scratch? Go hang out where your ideal audience already is and draw them into your audience with email marketing. Start building an email list using your lead magnet—a downloadable piece of information that people get for free in exchange for their email address. Remember, a lead magnet is a downloadable PDF, a quiz, or a workshop (live or evergreen). You should already have one tucked into your Radical Spark Signature Talk™.

PR is a wonderful way to capture an audience. Speaking in and of itself can be a PR activity. When you're on someone else's stage, they are vouching for you, giving you credibility, and allowing you to tap into their audience. Speaking is simultaneously a PR activity and a revenue stream—another reason I love speaking.

Spark Steps

1. Build Your Speaker Landing Page: After you've put together your media kit, create a dedicated page on your website specifically for your speaking engagements. Include your brand script, reels, testimonials, speaking topics, and booking information.

2. Choose Your Social Media Platforms: Pick one or two social media platforms where your ideal audience hangs out and post regularly about your signature topic and business. Develop a content strategy with three to five main subject areas.

3. Create Video Content: To effectively engage your audience, incorporate videos of yourself speaking and sharing ideas into your social media strategy.

4. Leverage PR Opportunities: Reach out to online publications, podcasts, and news outlets to get your message in front of their audience. Use their platforms to draw people into your audience.

5. Start Building an Email List: Use a lead magnet to capture email addresses and build a relationship with your audience through email marketing.

Remember, I am here to help! Head to the Spark Box at www.aleyaharris.com/spark-box for tools to support your marketing. You can also book a one-on-one marketing review session with me. On that call, we'll go over all of your marketing so that you feel confident you are putting your best foot forward.

Want to see what other budding speakers are doing to market themselves? Sign up for Spark the Stage™ at www.aleyaharris.com/spark and see what members of the community are doing to grow their speaker businesses.

.

Chapter 32

Contracts & Getting Paid

"When you undervalue what you do, the world will undervalue who you are."
—Oprah Winfrey

All right, now the rubber is meeting the road, and we are about to get paid. But before we do, we have to make it legal. You need to make sure that you sign a speaking agreement or a contract with every event that you speak at. Making sure everything is legal needs to happen whether you are getting paid or not. The speaking agreement is crucial for detailing how much you're getting paid and when. It also protects you from liability should any issues arise, such as travel problems or illness.

I will share some of the things I ensure are included in my speaking agreements.

Disclaimer: This does not constitute legal advice. I am not a lawyer, nor do I play one on TV. You should consult your lawyer for legal advice.

1. Basic Contract Stuff: Ensure that your contract includes standard clauses like indemnification, force majeure, liability, arbitration agreements, and your status as an independent

contractor rather than an employee. These are essential to protect your interests.

2. Event Details: Specify the event date, time, and location. Ensures that the contract is explicitly tied to a particular engagement, preventing any confusion or misuse of the agreement for other events.

3. Tools and Equipment: List what tools and equipment the organizer will provide, such as a projector, computer cords, slide clicker, lighting, etc. Also, make sure it mentions that dedicated AV support will be available at least 30 minutes before your presentation and, ideally, throughout the entire presentation if needed.

4. Payment Structure: To help with cash flow and ensure I'm not left high and dry, 50% of my fee is due upon booking, and the remaining 50% is due seven days before the event. This structure not only smooths out cash flow but also provides a buffer for any last-minute travel changes or expenses.

5. Travel and Accommodation: Whether it's a flat fee that includes travel expenses or a separate arrangement, I like to book my own flights. If for some reason the organizer needs to book travel for me, I specify the class—at least business for international and economy plus for domestic. I include a qualifier for hotels like "rated four stars or higher on TripAdvisor."

6. Session Title: Include the title of your Radical Authentic Signature Talk™ in your contract. Being specific prevents any misunderstandings about what you'll be delivering.

7. Photo and Video Capture: It's essential to have pictures and videos of yourself on stage for promotional purposes. Negotiate this in advance and include it in your contract.

8. Non-Monetary Compensation: Sometimes, it's not all about the money. Negotiate for things like gift certificates, tickets to local experiences, or guaranteed introductions to key individuals in the audience. These perks can add significant value and opportunities for future engagements.

9. Favorite Things List: After someone signs my contract, I send them a list of my favorite drinks, foods, colors, flowers, etc. It's not an expectation that they must provide these, but it's a nice touch that helps event planners know how to make you feel welcome. Once I started providing this list, I started receiving the most lovely thank you presents.

Now, let's talk about how you get paid. My favorite way to get paid is in straight-up cash—speaker fees. These can vary widely, and you'll find that most speaker websites don't list fees because they can fluctuate so much. As a beginner, get comfortable with the number zero. You'll often need to start by speaking for free to build your reputation and capture video. Once you gain experience, you can charge anywhere from $1,000 to $3,000, then move up to $5,000 to $10,000 as your profile grows. Then, the sky is the limit. Of course, never limit yourself. Always reach for higher fees because you and your story are valuable.

In addition to speaker fees, consider other revenue streams like selling products in the back of the room (e.g., books, workbooks), running add-on workshops, or offering exclusive deals to the audience. This is how you can get paid whether the organizer pays you or not. You can also use your presentations to generate leads for your business. And don't underestimate the power of networking—often, it's the relationships you build that lead to the best speaking opportunities.

Above all, remember that speaking is not just about making money (although it is very nice). It's about delivering value, building your brand, and creating opportunities for future engagements. So, stand in your power, know your worth, and get paid what you deserve.

Spark Steps

- Consult a Lawyer or Purchase a Speaker Agreement Template: If possible, have a lawyer review your contract template to ensure all legal bases are covered and to provide peace of mind.
- Negotiate Non-Monetary Compensation: Think about additional perks you can negotiate, such as gift certificates, local experiences, or guaranteed introductions to key individuals.
- Outline Travel and Accommodation Needs: Specify your travel and accommodation preferences clearly in the contract, including class of travel and hotel ratings.
- Include Photo and Video Permissions: Ensure your contract allows for photo and video capture of your presentation for promotional purposes.
- Send a "Favorite Things" List: After your contract is signed, send event organizers a list of your favorite items to help them make you feel welcome.

- Prepare for Different Payment Methods: Be open to various payment methods and ensure your contract specifies how you will be paid (e.g., bank transfer, check, cash).
- Review and Update Regularly: Periodically review and update your contract template to reflect any new preferences or learnings from past engagements.

I am not a lawyer, but I do know some great resources for contract templates. Check out the Spark Box at www.aleyaharris.com/spark-box to get your speaker agreement handled economically.

Spark the Stage

A s we end this transformative journey, let's take a moment to reflect on all we've uncovered together. You've delved deep into the essence of who you are, unearthing your Radically Authentic Self and embracing the power of your unique voice. We've explored the art of storytelling, the importance of clarity in your message, and the techniques to captivate your audience with confidence and poise. You learned several frameworks to create your Radical Spark Signature Talk™, and you now understand how to get paid to speak on a stage.

Pat yourself on the back. You've consumed a lot of information and should be super proud of yourself!

This journey hasn't just been about learning how to speak; it's been about discovering the depth of your own story and understanding the profound impact it can have on others. By now, you should feel empowered, knowing that your voice matters and you have the tools to make a lasting impression from the stage.

In every great story, there is a call to action—a moment when the hero must step forward, face their fears, and embrace their destiny. This is your moment. I'm calling you to action on your hero's journey. You have the tools, the insights, and the confidence to step into your power and share your story with the world. The journey from underdog to hero is not just about you; it's about the countless others who will be inspired and transformed by your words.

It has been an honor to guide you through this process. Your willingness to be vulnerable, to dig deep, and to embrace your authenticity will reap boundless positive results and help you continue to add to your list of successes. Thank you for letting me be part of your journey. Your courage and commitment to growth have set the stage for incredible things to come.

The end of this book is just the beginning. If you're ready to dive even deeper, I invite you to join me in the Spark the Stage™ course. Here, we can work together to refine your skills, connect with a community of like-minded speakers, and receive personalized feedback to help you excel. Visit www.aleyaharris.com/spark to learn more and sign up.

If you've found value in what we've explored and believe others could benefit from hearing these insights, consider booking me to speak at your next event. Together, we can create transformative experiences for your audience. For booking inquiries, please visit www.aleyaharris.com and schedule a call.

Your referrals mean the world to me. If you know event organizers or platforms that would benefit from my message, please refer me. Spreading the word helps extend the reach of Radically Authentic Strategic Storytelling™, allowing more people to experience the power of true connection and transformation.

For more tools, insights, and resources to support your speaking journey, visit the Spark Box at www.aleyaharris.com/spark-box. This page will be continually updated with valuable content to help you stay on track and continue growing as a speaker.

As you close this book and begin your next chapter as a radically authentic professional speaker, remember your voice is powerful. Your story matters. By stepping into your authentic self and sharing your message, you have the ability to inspire, uplift, and transform. Don't wait for the perfect moment—create it. The world is waiting to hear what only you can say. Embrace your journey, take the stage, and spark the change you wish to see. Thank you for being a part of this incredible journey. Now, go out there and shine.

Meet the Author

Aleya Harris is a transformative force in the world of strategic storytelling and professional speaking. As the founder and CEO of The Evolution Collective Inc. and lead trainer of Spark the Stage™, Aleya combines her experience as a marketing executive and ex-Google Vendor Partner with her passion for helping others find their authentic voice.

A two-time Speaker of the Year award recipient, Aleya has delivered over 100 presentations and been featured on more than 125 podcasts. She's also the host of the award-winning *Flourishing Entrepreneur Podcast*. Her unique background, which includes a stint as Stevie Wonder's private chef and transformative Ayahuasca experiences in the Amazon, informs her multifaceted approach to storytelling and leadership.

In her debut book, *Spark the Stage: Master the Art of Professional Speaking and Authentic Storytelling to Captivate,*

Inspire, and Transform Your Audience, Aleya shares her expertise in turning personal experiences into compelling messages that resonate with listeners. This guide offers practical strategies for overcoming fear, inspiring audiences, and developing as a confident, authentic speaker.

With a background in various storytelling methodologies and a holistic approach to personal development, Aleya's insights have been featured in Thrive Global, Authority Magazine, and the Marketing Made Simple podcast. Through her work, she continues to inspire leaders and teams to embrace their unique narratives and create lasting impacts in their industries.

.

Made in United States
North Haven, CT
20 August 2025

71868517R00163